Ancient Lights

'D'you ever look in the mirror and you don't recognise the person looking back at you?'
Tom Cavallero, Hollywood actor, and his girlfriend Iona
are spending Christmas in England with his oldest friends,
Bea and Kitty. Bea's new lover, Tad, would rather hole up
quietly with his copy of *Pathology For Beginners*. Her daughter
Joni would rather be in Shepherd's Bush. Northumberland
in a blizzard isn't quite what Tom was expecting. And how
can anyone relax when Iona's filming their very move?
She's making a documentary about 'the real Tom'. But who
is that exactly? And what's out there in the garden that
disturbs them all so much? Tom, Bea and Kitty go back a
long way. They've known each other since they were young
and unformed. But who have they become? And what price
have they paid?
'Kitty, you're the realest person I know.'
'Tom, when was the last time you touched base with real?'

Shelagh Stephenson was born in Northumberland and
read drama at Manchester University. She has written five
original plays for radio, one of which, *Five Kinds of Silence*,
won the Writers' Guild Award for Best Original Radio Play
of 1996 and the Sony Award for Best Original Drama, and
is now a highly acclaimed stage production. Her first stage
play, *A Memory of Water*, opened at the Hampstead Theatre
in 1996 and transferred to the West End, where it won an
Olivier Award for Best Comedy in 2000. Her second play,
An Experiment with an Airpump, which opened at the
Hampstead Theatre, won the Peggy Ramsay Award in 1997
and played at the Royal Exchange Theatre, Manchester.

'An acute and funny writer, Stephenson carves out a
welcome territory that is distinctive, contemporary and
theatrical.' *Independent*

by the same author

The Memory of Water & Five Kinds of Silence
An Experiment with an Airpump

Ancient Lights

Shelagh Stephenson

Methuen Drama

Published by Methuen Drama

1 3 5 7 9 10 8 6 4 2

First published in 2000 by Methuen Publishing Limited

ISBN 13: 978-0-413-76070-8

Ancient Lights

Ancient Lights was first performed at the Hampstead Theatre on 29 November 2000. The cast was as follows:

Tom	Don McManus
Bea	Joanne Pearce
Kitty	Gywneth Strong
Tad	Dermot Crowley
Iona	Ruth Gemmell
Joni	Sheridan Smith

Director	Ian Brown
Designer	Tanya McCallin
Lighting	David Hersey
Sound	Nicholas Gilpin

Characters
Tom
Bea
Kitty
Tad
Iona
Joni

Act One

A black void bursts into life with the sound of wild talk-show applause, cheering. Back projections of flickering black-and-white stills and grainy video images of **Tom Cavallero** *in various film roles, publicity shots. The images are jumbled and constantly changing. They wash over the set, distorting it, disguising it and blurring its boundaries. Spotlight up on* **Tom**, *slumped in a swivel leather armchair, floating in a sea of himself. He's wearing dark glasses, expensive casual suit, open-necked shirt, light tan, stubble. He looks like what he is: an American movie star. He's slumped in laid-back, chat-show pose, raises a hand in recognition of the applause, smiles at the audience with a kind of lazy bewilderment and delight. The applause dies down.*

Tom   Thank you very much . . . Thank you . . . Hey, who says the British are tight-assed? Am I allowed to say that on TV? Excuse me? . . . My pleasure, totally, it's great to be here, Michael. I love England. I did a couple of years here as a student and I totally fell in love with just about everything. That whole experience has kind of resonated down my life, you know? I always knew I'd come back, it was just a matter of when . . . I mean, like, to stay a long while . . . maybe take a house . . . Excuse me? . . . I'm over to see some old college friends actually . . . we were like the three musketeers, shared a house for two years, me and two women, knew each other inside out. Still do. It's good to get together occasionally . . . I remember this thing from like twenty years back for some reason, I've never forgotten it. I was walking along a river bank in England this time, on a beautiful breezy summer's day, and there was an old house right there on the towpath, with chestnut trees and honeysuckle, and roses falling over the gate, and on the side of the house, high up, near the roof, was a wooden sign that said 'Ancient Lights'. And it struck me like a poem, like an echo of something long gone, kind of pagan and all tied in with this old, old river and this tumbling greenery, and it's just, I guess, kind of stayed with me, it's kind of reverberated inside of me all these years, you know . . . Excuse me? Sorry, sorry, I just got in from LA, so I'm a little tired, a little slow on the uptake. Have you tried melatonin? Some kind of mineral or vitamin or maybe it's an herb. I don't think it's chemical. Something to do with your pineal gland. It kind of takes the edge off jet lag. I'm double-dosing. Maybe I should triple-dose. There's some other thing where you shine a light at the back of your knee, d'you know if that works? But right, yeah, the weather . . . well . . . it's pretty scary after California, but I kind of like it. Real snow. I haven't seen snow for, like, ten years. I mean, I can't believe it. Real fucking snow . . . Well, what can I say?

Big Sky . . . yeah . . . it did pretty good business in the States, so we're hoping, you know . . . Right, I play Joe Washington, he's a paraplegic forensic guy whose marriage is in a mess and he's drinking too much and there are some really weird killings going on and you know he gets to thinking . . . I don't know, basically I play a cripple in an Armani suit who gets to have sex with a lot of women.

Snap blackout, snap lights up on:

Evening. Softly lit uncluttered, space, suggesting a large room. (Maybe one large Georgian window?) In the corner, a huge, half-decorated Christmas tree. One kitchen chair, and lots of large floor cushions, rugs. **Bea**, *fortyish, is sitting amid a pile of recipe books, fruit and vegetables, and a large uncooked goose.* **Tad**, *fiftyish, is sitting in the chair, reading. A bottle next to him.*

Tad   Did you know that at the moment of death, there might be an involuntary emission of semen?

Bea   I didn't, no. D'you think these chestnuts are organic?

Tad   And partially digested food might be regurgitated –

Bea   Jesus, what are you reading?

Tad   It's a sort of Pathology for Beginners. What happens when you cop it. Also you get an involuntary release of waste products. In. .iunta. ;. I love that. Death means never having to say you're sorry. And then, quite shortly after you're dead, depending on the weather, you take on a sort of greenish tinge –

Bea   Depending on the weather?

Tad   If it's hot it happens quicker, anyway, that's your gases and your fluids breaking down, and dispersing through the body. And then shortly after that you begin to smell –

Bea   Chestnut-and-prune stuffing, what d'you think? Although I'm worried about the prunes –

She looks at the packet.

Sulphur dioxide, what's that? No wonder fish are growing penises and everyone's got cancer –

Tad   Not that you get much experience of stinking corpses these days, it's all sleight of hand, they whisk you away and shove you in a fridge before you know you're even dead –

Bea *looks at the goose.*

Bea   I suppose I'll have to cook this on a rack, there's so much fat, although it says here you can freeze it –

Tad   You should live with a body, sit with it, have a wake, you know –

Bea   – frozen goose fat, what would you do with it, I mean, how much cassoulet can you eat –

Two telephones ring at once. **Tad** *picks up the one nearest to him, while* **Bea** *searches frantically for her mobile.*

Tad   Hello, Charnel House here . . . no, sorry . . . Charnel
. . . you know, the place they . . . right, right . . . sorry . . .
this is Thaddeus . . . hi, no, we've not met . . . no . . .

Bea *has found her phone. She has a phone voice which is slightly
grander than her normal one.*

Bea   Hello?

Tad (*to* **Bea**)   It's Kitty –

Bea (*hand over receiver*)   Ask her what train she's getting.
(*Back to mobile.*) Sorry . . .

Tad   Did you hear that?

Bea (*into mobile phone*)   Max, there's going to be a problem
with those questions for Tom, I just know there is. He won't
talk about his private life . . . I know, I know it's hard to
avoid it but basically can you just go easy on the stuff about
the underage sex?

Tad (*still talking to* **Kitty**)   Would you like me to come and
get you? . . . You what? . . . I should warn you though, I'll
have probably had a few jars by then . . . You what?

Bea   OK, OK, OK, but he really is worried about the
picture shoot . . . I mean, I might be able to persuade him
but what we have to avoid is anything remotely *Hello!*
magazine. No toxic technicolour, OK? No showing you
round his lovely toilet with en suite jacuzzi.

Tad (*picking up the bottle and looking at the label*)   Have you
ever tasted this stuff . . . 'Sercial Madeira' . . . it's called . . . I
could live on it . . . Oh right, I'm with you now . . . Second
left after Burnside Farm, no, you have to go through
Rothbury . . .

Bea   OK, Max . . . pleasure . . . and to you too . . .

She puts the phone down.

Tad   Right, see you tomorrow –

He puts the phone down.

She'll be here just after lunch.

BEA (*looking at her watch*)   Right. Everything's more or less on schedule . . . all that's worrying me now is did I pack the oyster knife –

She rifles through her bags.

Tad   In cold weather like this, a body can stay recognisable for several months if the coffin's sturdy, did you know that? If you're not in a coffin of course, if you're out in the open, foxes and that sort of thing will be after snacking off you. They always say in the papers, don't they, 'the body had been disturbed by animals'. Have you noticed how delicate the language of death is? It's like ballet. You have to do the whole thing on tiptoe. If they just said 'eaten', we'd know where we were.

Bea   When Tom and Iona get here, d'you think you could lay off the pathology for a while?

Tad   Iona. Jesus. She's not a crystal clutcher, is she?

Bea   Off-limit topics include death, dying, mortuaries, post mortems and bizarre funeral rituals. Also decay, putrefaction and bodily fluids.

Tad   They might be interested.

Bea   They won't.

Tad   It's research.

Bea   It's unhealthy.

Tad   If he's such a regular guy, as you keep saying, why are you so worried about me upsetting him?

Bea   Because it's important that this visit goes well. Trust me, it's extremely important. And because he's coming here for a rest, and he might have been into a lot of different things in his time, but as far as I know necrophilia's not one of them.

Snap blackout. Snap lights up on **Tom**, *same position as before, same projections, still doing his talk-show routine. He leans forward confidentially to the audience.*

Tom   Listen, can I just be straight with you guys? Can I do that, Michael? I just want to like really lay it on the line here . . . about the . . . with regard to . . . the situation I find myself in, which you might be wondering about in some way. Because of the newspapers and so forth. So. Right, OK. Let me just be completely straight and honest here. No bullshit, no pre- whatever, prevaricating. Just the fucking – excuse me, just the truth.

He swigs a glass of water.

First. It's taken this woman ten years to lodge this complaint. I mean, come on. Yeah, I slept with her. I had a brief relationship with her. Like three weeks. So what? Because, second, she told me she was twenty. She looked twenty-five. No way did she look sixteen. She had breast implants for Christ's sake –

The images vanish, as **Iona** *comes in with a camcorder to her eye:* **Tom** *is sitting in his chair with some hand luggage at his feet, blinking at her.*

Iona   Time to go, Tom, come on. We have one hour to get to the airport.

Tom *looks at the camera.*

Tom   Is that turned on?

Iona   What do you think?

Tom (*trying to laugh*)   Iona, come on . . . are you shooting this?

Iona *laughs.*

Iona   Were you talking to yourself just now?

Tom   No, I was running through some lines –

Iona   What lines?

Tom   Is there tape in that?

Iona   We've got an hour. The car's waiting.

Tom   Iona –

Iona   I'm not shooting you I'm just fooling around –

Tom *looks at his feet and then round the room.*

Tom   What happened to my shoes?

He begins searching for his shoes. She follows him with the camera.

Iona   A day in the life of a movie star, what did I tell you, it's just work work work, he's running through lines and he hasn't made a movie in six months –

Tom   Yeah, very amusing, I thought you said it wasn't going to be ironic –

He locates his shoes.

Iona   So, he's found his shoes, he's putting them on those beautiful, tan, pedicured feet – show us your feet, Tom –

Tom   Take a hike –

He goes to the door.

Iona   OK, some other time with the feet. And now, he's got his shoes on, he's going to the door – but no – he's remembered the hand luggage – he's turning back, he's picking it up – hold on, he's hesitating – should he leave it for the bellhop? OK, what the fuck, he'll take it himself, he's a regular guy – honey, talk to me, will you?

Tom   Iona, I thought there was a car waiting –

Iona   Just tell us why we're going to England, will you –

Tom   Who is 'us'?

Iona   The people who'll be watching the movie –

Tom   You said it wasn't turned on –

Iona *flicks a switch.*

Iona   It is now.

Tom *forces a smile, and goes into professional mode.*

Tom   We're heading for England, for a little Christmas break. We're going to promote my movie, to get a little spiritual peace, to get away from . . . all sorts of stuff basically, to see my oldest friends . . .

He looks at his watch.

Honey, I think we have to get out of here –

Iona   OK, OK.

She turns off the camera.

You're going to England to find your true self. That's what you said last night.

Tom   Last night I was drunk.

Iona   Hey, and today you're not?

Tom   How else do I ever get on a plane? We're not just talking scared here, scared doesn't even begin to approach what I'm going through, we're talking cold sweat, heart-stopping primal oh my God we're all going to die terror –

Iona   This is just ridiculous –

Tom   I know it's ridiculous, I know it is –

Iona   You have to get over the idea that planes only stay in the air because passengers will them to. It's technology, Tom. Some really smart people figured it out.

Tom   Look, can we just get out of here? Can we just get on the plane so I can take a sleeping tablet and wake up in London? So if we do fall out of the sky and into the ocean, I'll be unconscious before I hit the water.

He goes out. **Iona** *puts the camera to her eye.*

Iona   And he's leaving the room, heading for the lobby, the limo, then the airport, leaving behind the Pacific Ocean, the Californian sun, the beautiful women with virtual breasts and bonded teeth and native spirit guides. Heading for England where no one's heard of orthodontists and they're having the worst winter in living memory. And where he's aiming to find his true self. My God. What is this man on?

Snap blackout. Simultaneously snap lights up on **Tad** *and* **Bea** *almost as before, but next day, around lunchtime.* **Tad** *is lying on a cushion, reading and drinking whisky. The goose in now on the chair.* **Bea** *is using a hairdryer on it.* **Tad** *is reading his book.*

Bea   It helps to make the fat crisp.

Tad   There's a type of white fatty substance –

Bea   Well, it works with duck anyway –

Tad   – you find it in bodies that have been buried in damp spots, it's called adipocere, listen to this –

Bea   God, if Tom's gone vegetarian I'll cut my throat –

Tad   – 'the corpse had been submerged in shallow, cold water for at least three months' –

Bea   Last time I saw him he could only eat bananas, peanut butter and turkey, plus eight litres of water a day, I hope he's given that up –

Tad   – 'wrapped in polythene, and weighted down with rocks' –

Bea   – maybe I should make a nut loaf, just to cover all eventualities –

She turns off the hairdryer.

Tad   – 'it had also been partially eaten, in the exposed parts, by aquatic life' –

Bea   Tad, why are you so obsessed with what happens to you after you're dead? Why d'you want to know these things?

Tad   Why d'you want to not know? Anyway, it's research.

Bea   For what?

Tad   I think the new book's going to have a pathologist in it.

Bea   So suddenly you're moving into genre fiction? When did this happen?

Tad   It's more in the line of a philosophical investigation. Did Tom really sleep with a twelve-year-old?

Bea   Sixteen-year-old. She said she was twenty. And I could wring her neck for starting all this, the little shit. I've put an embargo on all newspapers for the duration. So don't you dare bring it up, OK?

Tad   All right, all right –

Bea   All that I require for inner happiness is that things run according to plan –

Tad And you live next door to an incredible delicatessen that sells arcane bits of dried this and that from a single backyard in an obscure region of Italy. I mean, bottarga, what the hell is it?

Bea – I don't need shrinks, I don't need yoga or shiatsu or Rolfing. I need a coherent schedule that runs seamlessly and without hitches. That is the true meaning of the word contentment. Bottarga is dried fish roe. And you've made a complete mess of that tree.

Tad It's not finished yet, I got sidetracked.

He gets up and begins to rearrange the tree haphazardly. **Bea** *opens another recipe book.*

Bea I don't know what he's going to make of it when he gets here. I tried to tell him Northumberland wasn't like Surrey, which is essentially a golf course, and that's the only bit of English countryside he knows. This weather'll kill him. They're snowed in up on the moors, they're dropping hay bales by helicopter.

Somewhere, a phone rings out the '1812 Overture'. **Bea** *picks up the mobile. It's not that.* **Tad** *looks round puzzled. She looks under cushions, empties her bag.*

Tad Have you bought another bleeding phone?

Bea Fuck –

She rushes out. **Tad** *pours himself some more whisky. He takes a chocolate star off the Christmas tree, eats it and goes back to his book.* **Joni** *comes in looking like Bambi. She's wearing a skimpy cardigan with a tiny skirt and a lot of eye make-up.*

Joni Got a cigarette?

Tad Your mother doesn't like you smoking.

Joni It's Christmas.

Tad I don't have any.

Joni Liar.

She goes to his jacket and takes out a packet and lighter. Lights up.

Tad Well, that's it. You'll get cancer and die.

Joni You'd like that. You could use me as research for your next book.

Tad Fame at last. You'd love it.

The phone stops ringing.

Joni Yeah, I would actually. But only if I recovered. It played 'Annie's Song' when she first got it, you know.

Tad What?

Joni The phone. She's reprogrammed it. D'you realise she's got six different numbers now? When she dies, I'm going to get her a headstone in the shape of a telephone. And on it, I'm going to write: 'Sorry I can't take your call right now.'

She shivers.

I'm freezing, aren't you?

Tad You don't think that might have something to do with what you've got on?

Joni It's this stupid house. I hate it up here. It's full of sheep. It's freezing. It's crap. Why couldn't we just have stayed in London?

Tad Your mother and her roots. You know what she's like.

Joni She comes from a council house in Whitley Bay. What's a Georgian mansion got to do with her roots?

Tad   You don't really get the notion of landscape and memory if you come from Hammersmith.

Joni   Whitley Bay doesn't have landscape. It has amusement arcades. Anyway, I can't stand landscapes. I like streets and cinemas and department stores and lights. Thank God I'm going to Dad's on Boxing Day. I'm going to refuse to come next year. Did you see me on the telly?

Tad   When?

Joni   At the weekend. Did Mum not tell you? They were doing this news thing because you know that boy in year ten brought three hand grenades to school, and so they sent cameras and everything, and I was just hanging around with loads of other girls, and they interviewed me. And the cameraman said afterwards that there are two types of people: those whose skin absorbs light and those whose skin reflects it, and I reflect and that's the best. That's what all the movie stars have. He said I looked luminous. He had really horrible teeth though.

Tad   How old was this cameraman?

Joni   About as old as Mum. But not as ancient as you. Are we going to be in this film, d'you think?

Tad   What film?

Joni   That Tom's girlfriend's making.

Tad   What's it about?

Joni   Him.

Tad   Why, what's he done?

Joni   God, you're so irritating.

Tad   Are you thinking of auditioning then? D'you think you might wow them with your new-found luminosity?

Joni   I've met him before, you know.

Tad   I know.

Joni   Aren't you going to ask me what he's like?

Tad   No.

Joni   He's really handsome but dead normal. His eyes are exactly like mine. Except he's got a kind of aura thing, you know?

Tad   Ah right. A class of archangel.

Joni   He makes your throat go dry. You can't think of anything to say. You feel like you might faint or something.

Tad   I can't wait.

Joni   But I was really really immature then, I hadn't even started my GCSEs or anything.

Bea *comes back.*

Bea   Right, the cab got lost but Kitty's on her way. Tad, keep off the subject of death, and, Joni –

She takes her cigarette and stubs it out.

Joni   Mum, it's my right to get cancer if I want to, OK? God . . .

She stomps out.

Tad   Did you know the suicide rate soars at Christmas? All those poor fuckers quietly sawing through their wrists in front of *The Sound of Music.* I bet you the murder rate goes up too.

Bea   Tad.

Tad   Sorry.

She goes to the tree, pushes him out of the way and starts to sort it out herself.

So. Kitty. What's she like then?

Bea   I met her in the registration queue my first day at university. She was wearing an army greatcoat, and I had an Afghan. Neither of which had been seen in London since before the Boer War. I saw her in the queue looking self-conscious, and my heart leapt: oh thank God, I thought, someone else who's got it wrong and knows it. We can form a gang. We both read English, and both went into journalism.

Tad   So why didn't you stick it?

Bea   She went the serious route. I got sidetracked. One minute you're trying to be Martha Gellhorn and the next you're at a party with a glass of champagne, interviewing someone about kitten heels and having her pubic hair waxed by some woman who comes over from New York every other Thursday but she's booked up for a year. And they're paying you loads of money for it and you've never had any before. You kind of get caught up.

Tad   God, you're exotic. That was probably around the time I had a temp job, administering ECT treatment at St Columba's Psychiatric Unit.

Bea   Jesus, you've had some weird jobs.

Tad   The pork-pie factory was worse.

Bea   Anyway it dawned on me that what I was doing was essentially PR, and that I was better at it than most of the people I was dealing with. Of course Kitty thinks what I do is trivial and stupid because it involves socialising and parties.

Tad   A reasonable proposition.

Bea   Actually it's bloody hard work, it requires enormous diplomacy, and phenomenal organisational skills. Neither of which are Kitty's strong points, I think even she would admit that.

Tad   'Good evening. I'm fierce, I'm tough, I'm uncompromising. I go where grown men fear to tread. I don't take no for an answer and I'm standing here, surrounded by machine-gun fire and mortar bombs, wearing a bulletproof vest and no mascara. Mess with me if you dare. This is Kitty Percival, BBC News, Kosovo.'

Bea   She doesn't do that any more. She's presenting a series about road accidents.

Tad   I bet she's seen loads of bodies, has she?

Bea   It's all reconstructions. She's not filming real accidents for Christ's sake.

Tad   I mean, when she did wars.

Bea   This death jag you're on, are you doing it expressly to irritate me?

Tad   No. People think that sex is the thing that really gets us going. The old Freud bollocks. But it's not, it's death. That's the lad that drives us on –

Bea   Have you been eating these chocolate stars?

Tad   No –

Bea   There's supposed to be fifty, and there's only thirty-seven. Tad, these stars are covered in real gold leaf –

Tad   Well you're an arse for buying them then, aren't you, but listen –

Bea   – I wanted fifty, not thirty-seven –

Tad   – if death wasn't looming out there, you'd never get out of bed in the morning. If you're a painter or a writer or a pathologist, you do what you do because of your attitude towards death. Art's bound up with it, success is bound up with it. D'you not think that?

Bea   No. It's not the sort of thing I think about.

Tad   I'm forcing myself to face the absolute, objective reality of dying. What's wrong with that?

Bea   If you're thinking of it as an inoculation, I have to tell you you're doomed to failure –

Tad   De Gaulle took a quarter of a grain of arsenic every day, did you know that? To prepare himself for the poisoned croque-monsieur he was expecting any moment.

Bea   All it is in your case, is obsessional morbidity.

Tad   Look, I'm not into digging up body parts and making them into pendants. I don't want to be sleeping in cemeteries so I can be closer to the dead –

Bea   Thank Christ for that –

Tad   There are people who do that, you know, ask any policeman about the number of people who sleep in graveyards because they like it –

Bea   Why do you know such weird, sick things?

Tad   I read a lot.

Bea   Why can't you read *Hello!* magazine?

Tad   I don't need to. I live with you. Look, I'm writing about a pathologist. A pathologist opens up a body and tries to find the story of a life that leads to a death. He's looking for patterns and signs and hidden disturbances, he's looking for a story, right –

Bea   Are you frightened of dying, is that it?

Tad   Of course I'm fucking frightened.

Bea   You've got years yet.

Tad   I'm at the age when I hear a wonderful piece of music and I don't think, great, I'll have that on my *Desert Island Discs*, I think great, I'll have that at my funeral.

Bea   I've always done that. I'm having 'Into the Mystic' by Van Morrison.

Tad   There you are, you're making preparations. Everybody does. We can all see the end of the road out there.

Bea   But what difference does it make to me if I go green after I'm dead?

Tad   Are you going to be cremated or buried, d'you think?

Bea   I've no idea. I'm not interested.

Tad   Ah come on, you must be.

Bea   I'm not. I'll be dead. I won't care.

Tad   If you care about your funeral music, you must care about where you're going to be while they're downing bottles of stout at the wake. Up the chimney or six feet under?

Bea   Tad, none of it matters because when you're dead things don't. In general, one of the things the dead don't do, is care. Now. Remember that new book programme?

Tad   Yes . . .

Bea   I spoke to them earlier.

Pause.

Tad   And?

Bea   I think they want you too. I wasn't going to tell you until it was a hundred per cent, but what the hell.

Tad   Oh. Right.

Bea   Is that all?

Tad   What d'you mean?

Bea   D'you know how many strings I had to pull to set this up? D'you realise how many people I had to take to lunch?

Tad   Ah Jesus, it sounds like hell –

Bea   People with Palm Pilots who've been on BBC management courses, people you'd rather die than spend an hour with under normal circumstances –

Tad   Sorry, no, I didn't mean it, it's fantastic, sure, it's great, it's just . . . ah fuck it, it doesn't matter.

Bea   What?

Pause.

Tad   I don't really like doing these TV shows, you know –

Bea   Oh, for God's sake, d'you want to sell any books or not?

Tad   Of course I do, it's just I keep thinking of that Faulkner thing, you know, 'It's my ambition to be, as a private individual, abolished and voided from history, leaving it markless, no refuse save the printed books.'

Bea   Well, it didn't work then, did it, because everyone's heard of Faulkner, but if you go on like this no one will ever have heard of you. I worked my arse off to get you this deal.

Tad   But I talk bollocks on those programmes.

Bea   A) That's not true, and B) even it was, who cares? You're out there, in the public eye, you're visible and that's all that matters.

Tad   I'm not sure I'm so keen on this visibility thing.

Bea   If you're invisible, you might as well be dead, I'm sorry, but that's the way it is.

Tad   Tolstoy never had to do this.

Bea   Tolstoy doesn't need to. He's the literary equivalent of Guinness. Not everyone's tried it, but everyone's heard of it. With you, we have to get your face on the screen, we have to get people talking about you otherwise, by this time next year, you'll be remaindered.

Tad   But the conversations you have to have. They're ridiculous. 'What were you trying to say in this book?' 'I thought you'd just read it?' 'I have.' 'So that's what I was trying to say.' Jesus. What do they want? Simultaneous translation? A parallel text? Anyway, the writer's the last person you should ask. What happens, right, is you get to the end of your book or whatever and you look at it and think, well, it seems to be a class of aardvark, and I'd a notion it might be more in the line of a mongoose. But there it is, what can I do?

Bea   That's why they want you on their programmes, because that's very entertaining.

Tad   But it's not true. I just made it up.

Bea   It doesn't matter if it's not true.

Tad   Why doesn't it?

Bea   Because it's a TV programme, it's entertainment, not moral philosophy.

Tad   Radio Four. I like that. Couldn't you get me on there? I bet you I'd be really radiophonic. People like Irish voices, there's loads of them on Radio Four.

Bea   Exactly –

Tad   Sure they'd love me.

Bea   Look, they love you because you're televisual.

Tad   And I'm a great writer.

Bea   That's secondary.

Tad   Are you saying I'm a crap writer?

Bea   No, of course I'm not.

Tad   Because I'm not interested in being some literary fucking pin-up –

Bea   You're not that good-looking.

Tad   I'm serious –

Bea   All I'm saying is charm sells. Count your blessings.

Joni *brings* **Kitty** *in, wrapped in huge coat, scarves, gloves etc.*

Joni   Mum –

Kitty *looks wan.*

Kitty   Hello . . .

Bea   Kitty! Thank God you got here. Tad, this is Kitty –

Kitty *bursts into tears.*

Bea   Jesus, what's happened? Are you OK?

Kitty *continues to sob.* **Tad** *pours her a drink.*

Tad   Have some whisky. Sit down. What happened?

He sits **Kitty** *in the chair.*

Bea   Kitty? What's wrong? What's going on?

She puts her arm around her. **Kitty** *heaves and sobs.*

Joni   Something to do with the taxi driver.

Kitty   The taxi driver . . . he . . .

She sobs.

Bea   He what . . . what did he do?

Joni   Shall I call the police?

Kitty (*sobbing*)   . . . he . . . he . . .

Bea   What? . . . Oh my God, what?

Kitty (*through sobs*)   . . . it's stupid . . . it's stupid . . .

Bea   No it's not, try to tell us, come on . . .

Kitty (*through sobs*)   . . . he shouted at me . . .

Tad   The taxi driver shouted at you?

Bea   He shouted at you?

Kitty (*through sobs*)   Yes . . .

They all look at each other.

. . . he called me a rich bitch because I only had a fifty-pound note and he didn't have any change . . .

She continues to sob. **Tad** *and* **Bea** *exchange a delicate look.*

Bea   Tad, she needs a large whisky –

Tad   I've just fucking given her one –

Bea   – She needs hot water in it, with honey and lemon –

She takes the whisky from **Kitty** *and goes out.*

Kitty   You must think I'm really stupid –

Tad   Not at all, here – (*Taking her coat.*)

Kitty (*sniffing*)   I've been having a really horrible time, I'm sorry –

Joni   There's a girl in my class who's really depressed and her doctor put her on Prozac –

Kitty (*looking round*)   Where's the furniture?

Tad   She got rid of it. All the cushions are full of organic hops.

Kitty   Jesus wept . . .

Tad   It was after she went to Morocco . . .

Bea *comes back.*

Bea   I've put the kettle on. Now. What's going on? What's with all the weeping? So a taxi driver shouted at you. Why didn't you shout back?

Kitty   I can't help it, I cry all the time, anything sets me off. He just refused point blank to give me any change and eventually I got so frustrated, I threw the money at him and said 'Oh, keep the fucking change, for Christ's sake, and a merry Christmas to you too, pal.'

Bea   How much was the fare?

Kitty   Fifteen quid.

Bea   You gave him a thirty-five-pound tip?

Kitty   He wasn't even nice to me then, the shit, he still didn't help me with my bags.

Bea   This is outrageous. I'm going to report him.

She picks up a phone.

Kitty   Don't, he'll lose his job.

Bea   I bloody hope so.

Kitty   Bea, don't, he's probably got fourteen children, and they'll end up as child prostitutes and it'll all be my fault. Because I've got a wallet stuffed with fifty-pound notes that I don't deserve.

Tad   Ah now, steady on there, Kitty. I think that's going a bit far.

Bea   You can't just go throwing money at people –

Kitty   It doesn't matter, let's just forget it.

Bea   It's insane, if everyone did that, the whole . . . I mean, the entire –

Kitty   – economy would collapse. No it wouldn't. There'd just be less poor people.

Bea   And less rich ones –

Kitty   D'you never look at people and think there's something unbalanced here that I should be so comfortable and they should be so desperate?

Bea   Kitty, he was a Geordie taxi driver, not a legless child beggar in Calcutta –

Kitty   But there's something not right. There's something out of kilter, I feel it all the time –

Bea *gives her a beady look.*

Bea   You're depressed, aren't you?

Kitty   No.

Bea   Any word from Duncan? Where exactly is he?

Kitty   Covering a civil war, and a famine, in that order. So at the very moment you're carving the goose, he'll be watching someone starve to death in front of his eyes.

Bea   She's depressed.

Tad   There you go, Kitty, concern about the world at large is no longer considered a valid response to the inherent contradictions of capitalism, it's just a sign your mental feng shui's up the pole.

Bea   You ask these impossible questions, Kitty, you've always been like this.

Kitty   Always been like what?

Bea   Why do some people have to sell their kidneys to pay the rent while someone else picks at an arugula salad before knocking off a little magazine article about pedicures, thus earning more in a minute than the other one earns in a year? This is what you do when you're depressed. Round and round, on and on. But life's unfair and horrible, and unspeakable things happen, but there's only so much you can do about it. If you think like you do, you go mad and have to check into very expensive clinics, which of course is one way of offloading a substantial proportion of the cash you're feeling so guilty about –

Tad   Some people become nuns. Or social workers –

Kitty   What's wrong with having a conscience –

Bea   It's this ridiculous fucking Catholic thing –

Kitty   It is not fucking ridiculous.

Tad   I'm with you there, Kitty, the Christian Brothers never did me any harm –

Bea   Joni, go and see if the kettle's boiled –

Kitty   What's fucking ridiculous about it?

Joni *goes out reluctantly.*

Tad (*desperately*)   Why don't we all have a drink and calm down –

Bea   What's the point of a conscience if that's all it is? Ooh, I feel so guilty, I've got far too much money –

Kitty   Well, we have –

Bea   So give it away, endow a charitable foundation, burn it, but stop blahing on about it –

Kitty   Oh, fuck off.

Tad   Come on now, Kitty, d'you take a drink?

Kitty   Anything except blue Bols, Malibu or crème de menthe – although I have been known –

Bea (*looking at her watch*)   How long have you been here? Ten minutes, and we've already reached the fuck-off stage –

Tad   Have you two always been like this?

Kitty   She threw a jug at me once. A big jug. With water in it.

Bea   It didn't actually hit you –

Kitty   It might have done –

Bea   You gave my cashmere jumper to a man who said he needed contributions to a strike fund –

Kitty   That was twenty years ago, why d'you always have to bring this up –

Bea   Look, can we stop this –

Kitty   You started it–

Tad   I thought you said you were best friends?

Bea   We are –

Tad   So shut up then –

They both turn on him.

Bea/Kitty Who asked you?

Tad Jesus, I was only saying calm down.

Joni *comes back with the hot toddy, hands it to* **Kitty**. **Tad** *pours himself a drink.*

Bea You behave as if I just loll around eating grapes all day while the world starves. But I don't do nothing. I organised a breast cancer charity ball last week.

Kitty Were you for or against?

Bea We all do what we can –

Kitty Organising a ball, for Christ's sake –

Bea Subject closed, OK?

Silence. **Tad** *picks up a bowl.*

Tad Anyone fancy a Twiglet?

Bea They're not Twiglets they're pretzels.

Tad Pretzel then.

Bea No.

Silence.

Kitty (*conciliatory*) The tree looks nice.

Bea No it doesn't. He ate half the decorations.

Tad Covered in gold fucking leaf. My insides are like Tutankhamun's tomb.

Kitty *sips her drink, sniffs. A phone rings. They all reach into bags and grope under cushions.* **Bea** *finds one, as does* **Kitty**.

Bea Hello?

It continues to ring.

Kitty Hello?

The ringing continues. **Tad** *picks up a phone. The ringing stops.*

Tad Hello? . . . Oh right . . . right . . .

He looks troubled, awkward. He looks at **Bea**.

Excuse me a minute, will you?

He goes out with his phone. **Kitty** *blows her nose.*

Kitty D'you cry a lot now? Seriously. I mean, more than you used to? Is it our age or something?

Bea I don't cry at all.

Kitty What, never?

Bea I can make a little dry grunty noise, but that's it. The last time I really gave it a go, it was like weeping sand. I can't do it.

Kitty I can't stop.

Bea Maybe you're having an early menopause –

Kitty Beggars, shabby people with inadequate footwear, people adding up all their items at supermarket checkouts, in case they don't have enough money, all that desperate arithmetic, I can't bear it. People casually glancing into trash cans, rubbing at scratch cards in newsagent's shops, it kills me. I've become emotionally incontinent. And it's getting worse.

Bea Depressed, what did I tell you? Go straight to your doctor and ask for a year's supply of Prozac.

Tad *comes back.*

Tad You're supposed to be depressed at Christmas. It's all part of the festive spirit.

Bea Who was that on the phone?

Tad   My aged dad.

Bea   In Dublin?

Tad   Where the fuck else would he be?

Bea   OK, OK, don't be so snippy. Kitty, don't be depressed, it's silly, your show's doing really well, it's on prime-time TV for God's sake.

Kitty   It's a pile of shite.

Bea   Eight point four million people watch it.

Kitty   Lots of people voted for Hitler, it doesn't make it a good idea.

Bea   Oh, stop being such a whingeing drip –

Tad   Have you ever thought of taking up counselling?

Kitty   Christmas carols. They slay me as well.

Tad   So the holiday's looking like a bit of a minefield then.

Kitty   And if I'm not weeping surreptitiously, I'm shouting at the television, or screaming at the radio.

Bea   So, no change there then.

Kitty   Every morning I wake up and yell at the *Today* programme: Shut up you smug, stupid, ill-informed, self-referential bastards, you tiny-minded bunch of dicks, God, I fucking hate you and your nasty, cynical, self-congratulatory world, your wall-to-wall opinionation about everyone and anything whether you know the first thing about it or not, jostling for your two minutes of airtime so you can tell us how you feel about the health service or teenage mothers or why the prime minister should be castrated because he smiles too much, and it doesn't matter what you say anyway because the interviewer is honour bound to disagree no matter what –

Joni (*off*)   Mum –

Tom *and* **Iona** *come in, followed by* **Joni**. **Iona** *is filming.* **Bea** *leaps up.*

Bea   Tom!

She goes over, beaming, and hugs him.

Tom   Hi, guys. We made it! We didn't die!

Kitty *is still streaked in teary mascara as she gets up and gives him a kiss.*

Kitty   Hi. How are you?

Tom   Great, we're great, good to see you, you all look terrific. You know the Brits are a very ugly race –

Bea   Thanks –

Tom   No, not you, I mean en masse, at Heathrow. I know in the States we do fat, but over here, I always forget. All these stumpy little pig folk –

Bea *pushes an awkward* **Tad** *forward.*

Bea   Tom, this is Tad, luckily, he's Irish –

Tad *is smiling for his life.*

Tom   Hi!

Iona   Hi, Tod!

Tad (*still smiling*)   Tad –

Tom *hands his coat and scarf to* **Tad**.

Tom   And this is Iona –

Iona *keeps filming.*

Bea/Kitty/Tad/Joni   Hi, Iona . . .

Iona   Hi, everyone . . .

Awkward pause. They all look at the camera.

Tom   She's making a documentary. Didn't I tell you?

Bea   Of course you did –

Iona   You're doing great so far.

Kitty   A documentary about what?

Tom   Me.

Bea   It's going to be shown on television.

Kitty   Are we in it?

Bea   Look, why don't you give me your coats, and sit down, it looks like a book launch –

She takes their coats and goes out.

Tad   Would you like a go of the chair?

Tom   What? Oh . . . no . . . I'll just . . . what happened to the furniture?

Kitty   Filled with organic hops. The cushions.

Tom   Really? Why is that?

Kitty   One of the great mysteries. Try sitting on one. It's like being trapped in a brewery. A brewery in a souk.

Tom *sits down on a cushion.*

Tom   Can someone get me some chocolate? I have low blood sugar.

Tad *looks around helplessly.*

Tad   Chocolate . . . chocolate.

Iona   Organic hops. What do they do?

Tad   Search me. I'm sticking with the chair.

Joni (*shouting*)   Mum? Have we got any chocolate?

Tad *grabs a handful of chocolate stars from the tree and gives them to* **Tom**.

Tom   What is this?

Tad   Chocolate. Covered in real gold leaf.

Tom   Isn't that dangerous?

Tad   Well, it hasn't harmed me.

Iona *trains the camera on the cushions.* **Kitty** *looks at* **Tom**.

Kitty   So you're making a film. And we're in it? Hey, thanks for asking us, Tom, thanks for the consultation –

Tom   Iona, maybe you can pick this up later –

Kitty   What if we don't want to be in it? What if we object?

Iona   Well, I film you objecting.

Tom   OK, Iona, just take a break for a while, come on –

Joni   Why don't you film me instead, I don't mind –

Iona *turns off the camera and puts it down.*

Iona   OK, look, I'm sorry, I should have warned you. Not too sensitive, I admit it. I just wanted to get the reunion bit, that's all, but now I have, and that's fine. I'll edit that little spat out.

Tom   And maybe edit the pig folk out, I don't want to erode my British fan base entirely.

Iona *holds out her hand to* **Kitty**.

Iona   Kitty, I'm really pleased to meet you, I've heard so much about you.

Tom   Yeah, it's great to see you, Kitty. I didn't know for sure you were going to be here.

Kitty   I wasn't. I had a – my plans fell through.

Tom   Great. Do we get to meet your husband at last? Douglas, is it?

Kitty   Duncan. He's covering a civil war. He might be being shot at this very moment. Which is one of the reasons I'm a touch tense.

Tom   Oh. Right. Hey. That's awful. But you don't look tense. You look great.

Kitty   Bollocks. I look a hundred years old.

Tom   I don't think I like this chocolate. Can someone get me something different? Like a muffin or something?

Joni   Mum, have we got any muffins?

She hurries out.

Tom   You look great, Kitty, because you're still in a furious rage about something, it's a relief, I'm sick of people mellowing, it's kind of depressing –

Kitty   I'm not in a furious rage –

Iona   I wish I was getting this on tape, it's so authentic.

Kitty   I'm sorry?

Tom   Iona's a postmodernist.

Iona   I mean authentic in the authentic sense, dick brain –

Tad   D'you take a drink, anyone?

Tom   I guess you'd know all about that, wouldn't you?

Tad   What? Drink?

Tom   Postmodernism. You're a writer, OK?

Tad *laughs inordinately.*

Tad · Oh, right, right, I'm with you, great, that's really funny . . .

Tom   It is? Why?

Tad   Oh, right, no. I don't even know what postmodernism is. I mean, I do but, you know, not consciously.

Tom   Right . . .

Tad   Yeah . . .

He laughs even more. No one else is a laughing. He stops.

Anyway.

Bea *comes back with a tray of champagne and Guinness, and some cakes for* **Tom**. **Iona** *turns on the camera again.*

Tom (*to* **Tad**)   She ever tell you we were all in a production of *The Seagull?*

Bea   I wasn't in it, I was the stage manager.

Tom   Kitty was Nina, and I was Konstantin. She mumbled and I shouted.

Kitty   I wasn't Nina, I was Masha. In mourning for my life.

Tom   Remember when Trigorin came on and the tree fell on him?

Kitty   And Bea shouting over the tannoy: 'Actor down, we have an actor down.'

Tom   You were lying in the wings saying 'I'm going to die, I'm going to die –'

Bea   And I got very cross with you, and told you it was unprofessional –

Tom That was the summer, remember, sitting up there on the roof, in pigeon shit, listening to Bruce Springsteen for the first time? D'you remember that blast? Tramps like us –

Bea/Kitty (*singing*) – 'Baby we were born to run, duh dang dang dang –'

Joni No, Mum, don't start, I'll be sick, honestly.

Iona Oh, sing it, go on –

Kitty Tom, what is this, why do we have to have this camera going?

Tom It's just a little film, you know.

Kitty Why?

Tom Why what? This muffin is weird.

Kitty Why are you making this little film?

Tom Well, because . . . you know . . . is this banana?

Kitty Because what?

Bea Kitty – I think it's bran or something, Tom –

Kitty No, I don't know what he means –

Iona This is great, you're so aggressive, no one's ever aggressive to Tom. No one ever says no to him –

Tom Iona, will you stop trashing me –

Iona He could go into a restaurant and ask for a little dry toast and a boiled baby, and they'd say, our pleasure, you got it, take a seat Mr Cavallero.

Tom This is Iona's film. Kind of *cinéma-vérité*. About me. My life. The real me or something. You know the kind of stuff.

Iona   A documentary, not a biopic. I mean, I hate biopics, we're not talking hagiography here. We're talking what it's actually like to be someone like Tom.

Kitty   Yes, but why?

Tom   Excuse me?

Kitty   Why d'you want to do that with your life? Why not, just, you know, have a life? Why d'you have to make a movie out of it?

Bea   Kitty, stop being a pain in the arse –

Tom   Because Iona makes documentaries, that's what she does. She did one about a vulcanologist who got engulfed, it was awful –

Iona   But it was incredible, I actually got it on film, the moment when the lava rolled right over him like something from the black lagoon.

Tom   We met when I went to judge her film school project –

Iona   And d'you know what he said about my piece? He said he it was a total mess –

Tom   I didn't mean it like that –

Iona   It was a mess, I was into alternative scenarios, randomness, weird timescales, you know when you're twenty-three and you just want to trash the world and put it back together in a different order –

Kitty   And what about now?

Tom   Now we're just making a movie. A little bit *cinéma-vérité*, but basically a movie.

Iona   Documentaries always pretend to be actuality, as if this was the way it happened. But they ask people to do things again, to say things they maybe don't mean, they edit stuff out, they splice it together to fit a preconceived notion –

Kitty   Whereas you're going to what?

Iona   I'm hoping it's going to be more truthful, that's all.

Kitty   I spend my life in front of cameras, Tom, I'm supposed to be on holiday –

Bea   Kitty, there's definitely something wrong with your hormones at the moment, you're being ridiculously bad-tempered –

Iona *turns the camera on* **Tad**.

Tad   No, no, don't train that thing on me –

Iona   Don't be so shy . . . come on . . .

Tad *tries to dodge away from the camera.*

Tad   If you point it at me long enough I'll confess to something –

Iona   Like what?

Tad   I don't know, anything. I'm a defrocked priest who used to be a woman. I cheated on my wife with a lesbian go-go dancer. I was born with three penises but now I've found love with a Dobermann pinscher. Cameras scare the fucking pants off me. God knows what I'll admit to.

Tom   You're a funny guy. You're great. I like you.

He looks at **Bea**.

Should I tell him?

Tad   What?

Bea   Go on.

Tad *looks suspicious.*

Tad   Tell me what?

Tom   I want to buy the film rights to *Plunket's Causeway.*

Tad (*floored*)   What?

Bea   He wants to play Padraig.

Kitty   I thought Padraig was a man in a tweed suit from Tipperary?

Tad *looks at her.*

Kitty   She sent it to me.

Tom   So, what d'you think?

Tad   Well, I . . . I mean . . .

Tom   OK, I know, you don't think I can do the accent, right?

Tad   No, no, I mean –

Tom   Guess where I was born?

Tad   Idaho? Palm Springs? Albuquerque? I give up.

Tom   County Down.

Tad   The Cavalleros of County Down?

Tom   I was going through my Robert De Niro phase. So listen, I'd be honoured, truly. I love your book, I mean that bit where the priest throws up on the deathbed, that is just so, anyway, I'm rushing ahead here, what d'you say, Tod?

Tad   Tad –

Tom   Didn't I say that?

Bea   Tad, could you try and sound a bit more thrilled?

Tad   I am, I am, I'm just, you know, a bit taken aback, but sure, it's great –

Tom   I thought we could do some research together in Ireland.

Tad   Right, that'd be great, yeah –

Tom   Can we shake on it? I mean I know we have to talk to your agent and stuff, but I'd be so thrilled –

Tad   Sure, right, OK –

*He shakes **Tom**'s hand, awkwardly.*

Tom   Slainte.

Tad   Great. Slainte.

Kitty   Congratulations, Tad –

Tad (*still awkward*)   Thanks.

Iona   Hey, Mr Hollywood –

Tad   Ah come on now. Take the camera away, can't you? Can a man not be thrilled in private?

A phone rings.

That's mine, excuse me, can you?

He hurries out with his phone.

Joni   Why don't you film me now? I don't mind.

Iona *moves the camera round to her. She gives it a sultry look.*

Joni   Hi, I'm Joni –

Iona *moves the camera round to **Bea**.*

Bea   Are you looking at me now? Oh, don't please, I hate it, I can't bear seeing myself, it's my teeth or something, and my little scrabbling hands, don't you hate that –

Kitty   I don't have little scrabbling hands –

Iona *keeps the camera on her, and* **Joni** *struggles to find a way to keep in the frame.*

Bea   You imagine you're rather composed and elegant and you see yourself on screen and you realise you're a twitchy little graceless person with a mouth like your mother's and huge fat arms –

Iona   You look great –

Bea   No, please, I hate it, I feel sick when I look at myself, I'm such a disappointment and completely the wrong age – no, no, especially sideways, I look like a malevolent tortoise with a grudge –

Iona   OK, OK, so listen, here we are, it's December twenty-third, we're in this beautiful house in Northamptonshire –

Joni (*desperate to get the camera back on her*)   Northumberland –

Iona   Which is near Scotland, right?

Joni   Yeah.

Iona   And they have the weirdest accent I ever heard. That guy at the airport, I thought he was Russian. Do it for us, will you, Bea?

Bea   What?

Iona   That accent. Northumberland.

Bea   I can't, honestly.

Joni   She can when she's drunk.

Bea   Look, could you point that at someone else, d'you think?

Iona   OK, OK, you don't feel easy with impersonations. So, tell us about yourself, Bea.

Bea   No, honestly, ask someone else. I don't like this, I really don't.

Iona   This is weird. What's with you guys? Ask your average American to talk on camera and he'll tell you his life story. You won't even tell me your name.

Tom   Come on, Bea, lighten up.

Bea (*briskly*)   All right. I help Tom out bit when he's in Europe, I'm in PR . . . So, anyway, we've known each other since college, and . . . that's about it. Ask someone else, I can't think of anything else to say.

Joni   God, Mum, you're so pathetic –

Iona *trains the camera on* **Joni**, *who beams gorgeously.*

Joni   Have you heard of Joni Mitchell? Some hippie chick my mum's obsessed with, anyway, I'm named after her, and when Mum gets drunk she always sings 'I could drink a case of you and still I'd be on my feet' –

Bea   Joni –

Joni   Which is really ironic because she's always lying on the sofa by this point, totally unable to move –

Bea   I hope you're going to edit this out –

Iona   You're very photogenic, Joni.

Joni   I've got a light-reflecting complexion. Also, I'm a Libra, which is supposed to be the most beautiful sign in the zodiac, well, that's what it says in this book I've got. I'm not really sure if it's true though –

Tad (*returning*)   It's not. The Elephant Man was a Libran.

Joni   This is Tad, my mum's boyfriend, he's a Celtic person who writes books. I haven't read any of them.

Kitty   Is this going to go on all night? I mean, do we at least get to sit on the lavatory in private?

Tom   I don't. Tell us what you've been up to, Joni.

Joni   I'm learning to play the guitar.

Tom   Really? That's great. I used to play the guitar.

Joni   Yeah, I know. I've written some songs. I'm going to form a girl band with my mate Nubs. I could play some of them for you if you want –

Bea   I think that's enough now, Joni, you've been absolutely fascinating but you can have too much of a good thing –

Tom   Maybe just wrap it up now now, Iona. It's kind of irritating after a while.

Joni   Shall I play my songs, Mum?

Bea   Not tonight, Joni.

Joni *exits.*

Iona   OK, guys, just carry on. You won't notice me if you just pretend I'm not here.

Kitty   How can you pretend there's not a camera in the room?

Iona   Just talk amongst yourselves. Stop being so self-conscious. Go on. Talk. Do what you'd be doing if I wasn't here.

Silence.

OK. Tod –

Tad   Tad –

Iona   What part of Scotland are you from?

Tad   I'm not Scottish I'm Irish. We've just had a long conversation about it.

Iona   Oh, I'm sorry, I get confused. I'm not so hot on British accents.

Tad   That's OK, I'm Irish.

Joni *comes back with her guitar.*

Bea   Joni, please don't play that now.

Joni   God, any normal mother would be proud –

Bea   It's very distracting, that's all, when there's a room full of people –

Joni *throws her guitar down with a crash, muttering.*

Joni   All right, all right, I'm not going to, OK? God, you're such a pain –

Bea   I think we need more alcohol –

She picks up a bottle desperately and refills glasses.

Tad   So how was the trip then, Tom?

Tom   Excuse me?

Tad   The flight, you know.

Tom   It was . . . a regular flight.

Tad   I bet you got on the plane and turned left did you?

Tom   Excuse me?

Tad   You'd be in first class.

Tom   Well . . . yeah . . .

Tad   So what's it like?

Tom   I'm sorry?

Tad   First class. I always go steerage. I always want to ask them if I can have a quick glance upstairs, you know, when I get on the plane. I mean, d'you get double beds and Filipino handmaidens and that sort of thing? Or just a polyester sleep suit and a copy of *Hello!* magazine?

Tom   Well, it's . . . OK . . . I mean, you don't get there any quicker. If the plane crashes you still die.

Tad   Have you ever travelled steerage?

Tom   Economy? Not for around twenty years.

Tad   It's the most disgusting and demeaning form of travel known to man.

Tom   Yeah, I guess . . . but it's kind of difficult for me, you know, because of my . . . because people kind of bug me . . . I mean, when I travel, I like to be left alone –

Kitty   Really? I like spending eight hours next to a man weighing seventeen stones, in a seat designed for a midget. Preferably next to the lavatories. I really really love that –

Tom   I mean, people can be weird, you know –

Tad   Yeah, yeah. Right. I know what you mean, fans and that kind of thing. They can drive you mad, can't they?

Joni   What would you know about it?

Tad   I've had experience of this sort of thing, not as much as Tom, obviously –

Joni *shrieks with laughter.*

Joni   Who'd be a fan of yours?

Bea   Joni –

Tad   I've done a book signing –

Joni   – in Croydon –

Tad   There were some very weird people there, I'm telling you –

Tom   Like they're over-friendly, you know, or they're really aggressive.

Tad   Yeah, exactly, I know exactly what you mean –

Tom *looks at him.*

Tom   I don't think you do.

Tad   Well, I –

Tom   You cannot begin to imagine what I mean.

Tad   No, obviously, I just –

Tom   One guy comes up to me in the airport, d'you remember this, Iona? He comes right up to me and says: 'Hey, pal, all your movies stink. So don't get superior with me. Plus, my dick is one hell of a size. So up yours, buddy.' I never met the guy before in my life.

Iona   Tell them about the sandwiches, Tom.

Tom   Oh Jesus, the sandwich, yeah. That was just weird.

They look at him expectantly.

Does anyone have a cigarette? And maybe another muffin, I still need sugar.

Bea (*going out*)   A muffin, a muffin –

Tom   Make it low fat –

Joni   Mum, you said he didn't smoke.

Tom   Tom Cavallero doesn't, but I do. You know what I mean?

Joni   Tad's got some –

She rushes to **Tad**'s *jacket and brings out the packet. Offers them to*
Tom.

Tom   D'you mind?

Tad   No, go on.

Tom *lights up.*

Tom   We're in New York this time. In a deli, right. So I'm
sitting eating my pastrami with French mustard, a side order
of latke and sour cream, because I'm depressed and I've just
trashed my diet sheet. I bite into my sandwich, OK, and I
think what the hell is this? And I take out of my mouth this
kind of paper streamer or something, about so long. I
unravel it and it says: 'Tom, I really want to fuck you. I
want to have your children.' I open up my sandwich and it's
full of messages, on little pieces of paper. And I look up and
the waitress opens her shirt and shows me her breasts. Just
for like a split second. I smile, I figure it's always best to
smile, in case they have a gun, and we get out of there
quick. And when I tell my therapist he doesn't believe me.
He says are you seeing these sort of messages anywhere else
right now? Like on billboards, for instance? Maybe in the
Wall Street Journal? So I fire him. Who needs a therapist who
thinks you're crazy?

Tad   That's a great story.

Tom   It's not a story, it's true.

Tad   No, I know that.

Tom   It really happened to me.

Bea *comes back with a plate of muffins.*

Tad   Yes, I know, I only meant, Jesus, there's a lot of
fucking mad people out there.

Tom   And all of them are attracted to me. Thanks.

He takes the muffins.

Bea   I think this happens to almost everyone in your position, Tom. It's not specific to you. By the way, supper's almost ready.

Tom   Listen, other people get schoolteachers from Wyoming, they get beautiful young women, they get movie buffs, what I get is psychotics. People who collect cake stands and thimbles, and musical dogs, they hold the world record for lying in bathtubs of maggots, they're nudists, they believe the government's bugging their bathroom. They're basically not the sort of people you'd have over for supper. And they love me.

Iona   They don't love you, they don't know you.

Tom   You mean if they did know me they wouldn't? Is that what you're trying to say?

Iona   They're in love with a construct, Tom. Does someone else want to take this, so I can be in it for a moment?

Bea *looks at her watch.*

Bea   Is anybody hungry?

Kitty   She's been cooking for three weeks–

Bea (*briskly*)   Because I think I should serve supper soon, I don't mean to be rude, Iona, but we need to eat. Joni, can you show Tom and Iona and Kitty their bathrooms?

Kitty   Wow, are we dressing for dinner?

Bea   I thought you might want to get washed that's all.

Kitty   OK, OK . . .

She gets up, as do **Tom** *and* **Iona**.

Joni   Follow me. Yours has got a really stupid bath, Kitty. It's pale green plastic . . .

She goes out, they follow.

Tom   How long? Fifteen, twenty minutes?

Bea   That's fine.

He goes. **Tad** *lights up a cigarette, edgily, as* **Bea** *tidies up glasses, etc.*

Tad   Did I make a complete eejit of myself? I did, didn't I?

Bea   You did do some over-enthusiastic laughing at one point –

Tad   I can't help it. Famous people turn me into a complete dick. Something happens when they come into a room. The molecules regroup, there's some sort of atmospheric shift. I talk shite.

He puts his head in his hands.

Over-enthusiastic laughing. Jesus. I'm a fifty-year-old published author, I've had an article about me in the *Independent.* Tom Cavallero walks into the room and I'm infantilised.

Bea   You could have sounded a bit more delighted about the film. A few monosyllabic grunts. What happened to your famous Celtic charm?

Tad   Bea, listen –

Bea   I mean, he wants to come over and meet your family and everything –

Tad   *Plunket's Causeway*'s not about my family –

Bea   No, he knows that, but he also knows it comes from somewhere in you –

Tad   Bea, would you ever just stop?

Bea   What is the matter with you? What's wrong?

Pause. **Tad** *looks at her for a long time.*

Tad   I don't know how to say this.

Bea   What is it? Tad I've got to get the supper sorted out –

Tad   Fuck the supper.

Bea   What!?

Tad   I have to tell you something, Bea –

Bea   What?

Tad   I mean, if I told you something . . .

Bea   Like what, for Christ's sake??

Tad   I mean, you know, if . . . I told you . . . something about . . . if I told you quite a big thing . . .

Silence.

Bea   What . . . ?

Tad   Or maybe it's not so big . . . I suppose it depends how you look at it –

Bea   Tad, cut to the chase will you?

Pause. **Tad** *is in an agony of indecision.*

Tad   I need to tell you . . . I can't not . . . I'm just, I mean, oh Jesus, oh Jesus, I can't do it . . .

Bea   What? Can't do what?

Silence.

What are you trying to say?

Tad   Nothing.

Bea   For Christ's sake! What are you trying to tell me?

A beat.

You've met someone.

Tad   No –

Bea   She's younger, she's thirty-two, she wants children. All that stuff you said about never wanting a family, you've changed your mind. She has no cellulite and pert breasts and you're leaving me. She has nine-inch hips and a flat stomach and a PhD. I knew this would happen, I was waiting for it, oh Jesus –

Tad   No, for fuck's sake! It's not that.

Pause. **Bea** *looks at him.*

Bea   Well, what is it then?

Long pause.

Tad   I'm not . . . what . . . I'm not . . . oh fuck . . . I don't know how to say this . . . I mean . . .

Pause.

Bea   What?

Pause.

Tad   I'm not actually Irish.

Pause.

Bea   What?

Tad   I'm not Irish.

Bea   I don't know what you mean.

Tad   I'll spell it out for you. I-am-not-Irish.

Pause.

Bea   I'm still not sure what you mean.

Tad   Jesus fucking wept. I'm not bleeding Irish.

Pause. **Bea** *is very confused.*

Bea   You mean you were born somewhere else?

Tad   I'm from Hull.

Silence.

Bea   I don't understand what you're saying. You were born in Hull, so what?

Tad   No. I am from Hull. D'you see what I'm getting at?

Bea   Not really, no . . .

Tad   But the thing is, I couldn't get anyone to publish my stuff when I set it in Hull. It's not sexy or something. I was on my uppers. I went to Ireland and dossed about. This was twenty years ago. And you know. Sort of slipped into it.

Bea   What?

Tad   Being Irish.

Bea   You 'sort of slipped into' being Irish?

Tad   That's just about the size of it.

Bea   But you're not Irish?

Tad *looks agonised.*

Tad   No.

Bea   So –

Suddenly the lights go out. It's pitch black.

Fuck! Tad, are you having me on?

Tad   I'm not codding you.

Tom (*off*)   What's going on?

Bea   Hang on. There are candles somewhere.

She stumbles around looking for candles. **Kitty** *appears in the doorway.*

Kitty   Does this happen often?

Bea   Is that you, Kitty? It's the weather. Go back upstairs. Where're those fucking candles . . .

Tom (*off*)   Is somebody going to fix this?

Joni *comes in.*

Joni   This house is pathetic, Mum.

Iona *and* **Tom** *appear, in bathrobes.*

Tom   Isn't there a maintenance guy?

Kitty   Oh, for God's sake, Tom –

Bea   Look, go and get dressed, they'll come on again in a minute –

Tom   It's black as fuck up there –

Bea   Tad, can I speak to you in private, d'you think?

Tom   Where're the fucking candles?

Iona   This is wonderful. I love it. Is this place haunted?

Tad *strikes a match.*

Tom   Iona, shut the fuck up.

Tad   It is actually.

Bea   Tad, I need to speak to you.

Joni   You mean there's something in the house?

Bea   Tad –

Tad   Not so much the house as the grounds. Out there, not in here.

Bea *finds a candle and lights it.*

Tad   That's what they say.

Bea   Stop it, will you?

She lights another candle.

Tom   What? What's out there?

Iona   When do we get some light back?

Bea   Oh for God's sake, it happens all the time, it's nothing. Tad –

Tom   This is medieval, you can't live like this, someone get it back on, will you?

Bea   Tom, stop panicking, it's OK. We're just going to sit in the dark for a while, that's all –

Tom   OK, OK –

Kitty   What's this story, Tad?

Bea   Kitty, please, I like ghost stories but not when they're about my own house, OK?

Tad   This one's really fucking weird. I was completely spooked when I heard it.

Tom   Will I be able to sleep? I mean, will I have to keep the light on all night?

Kitty   You'll be lucky.

Tad   Don't worry. Whatever it is, it's not in the house, it's outside. Can I get anyone a drink?

He goes round with the bottle. The candles flicker and gutter. They all look at him expectantly. He sits down on the chair and lights a cigarette. Silence.

Bea   So? I thought you were going to tell us one of your stories, Tad?

Tad   I thought you didn't want to hear it.

Bea   Oh, for fuck's sake, what's outside the bloody house?

Iona   Hold on, hold on –

She picks up her camera. Turns it on.

OK. Go.

Tad   Well, if you're sure you want to hear it . . . do we need another candle, d'you think?

Bea   Tad –

Kitty   Oh, for God's sake –

She finds another candle and lights it.

Tad   Maybe it's a bit too bright now.

He snuffs it out again. Then another. Leaves just one candle, which he holds, flickering in front of him.

That's better. So. Where was I?

Kitty   'It was a wild and stormy night –'

Tom   I'm feeling kind of spooked here.

Tad   I haven't started yet.

Bea   Well, bloody start then.

Tad   OK, OK. The story comes from before this house was built, when this was common land on the edge of the moors. So it's very ancient, it's as old as the land itself. It's not complicated. The place is visited by a fetch.

Tom Excuse me?

Tad A fetch. The wraith of a living person. A doppelgänger. You know, your uncle Arthur appears to you at the very moment of his death on the other side of the world. But this, right, is not quite the same thing. This is a much more unusual manifestation. Here, you meet your own self out there on the moors. Your own doppelgänger. According to this story, it's happened twice this century and a score of times in the past.

Kitty I don't get it.

Pause.

Tad In 1923, a man called Thomas Earlby was out walking his dog at about five o'clock on a December evening. So it was dark, the way it is in the country, no light except the moon which kept dipping behind clouds. And the moors, you know, are pitch black. There's a frost prickling the ground and the two feet and four paws crunch and crackle over the coarse tussocks. Crunch, crunch. Pad, pad. Suddenly the dog stops, and refuses to go any further. Earlby coaxes him: Come on lad, come on. But the dog starts whining, and giving little uncertain barks, and Earlby looks up and sees a vague, bluish light coming towards them across the moors. The dog cowers now. He won't move an inch. The light gets closer and Thomas Earlby makes out the figure of a man, carrying a lantern, with a strange glow the colour of moonlight. But the curious thing is that the man makes no sound as he comes towards them over the frozen ground. Earlby calls out 'Who's there?' But the figure keeps coming until it's only a few feet away. And Thomas Earlby is transfixed, rooted to the spot: for the man before him is his own self. But himself white-faced and gaunt, sick-looking, his lips drawn back from his teeth. And this other self beckons to Thomas Earlby. Beckons to him, like this . . . (*He beckons.*) The hairs stand up on the back of Earlby's neck and he turns on his heel and flees, the dog scurrying alongside him giving a low whimper. And when he gets home he tells his wife and his old dad, who lives with them, about what he'd encountered out there on the moors. And the father goes pale, and walks out of the room, goes upstairs to his bed, without a word. And the next morning Thomas Earlby is dead.

Silence.

Tom   But like . . . I mean that's not really a haunting, right? I mean, it's not like there's a ghost out there, right?

Tad   I wouldn't call it that, no. It's more that this is a place where such things occur. You meet your own doppelgänger who beckons you to your doom. Apparently. Maybe that's why it's called a fetch. Because it comes to fetch you. Your own self comes to fetch you . . .

He snuffs out the candle. Blackout.

Tom   Holy shit . . .

Act Two

Scene One

Later. **Bea** *and* **Tad** *are alone at last.* **Bea** *is in shock.*

Bea Tad, please tell me this Irish thing is an elaborate joke.

Tad It's not.

Bea But for Christ's sake . . . I mean . . . you sound . . . everything about you . . .

Tad I know. I'm spongy. I absorb stuff. And the whole thing of it is, I feel Irish. It's not as if it's hard for me. I mean, really, I might just as well be. Except I'm not. And you know, being on the television and all that. You putting me on all those programmes. It's only a matter of time before someone from Hull . . . you know . . .

Bea What . . . ?

Tad Recognises me.

Pause.

Bea I can't take this in . . . I mean . . . So who . . . ? Who the hell are you?

Tad Me. I'm still me, it's just, you know . . .

Bea But Thaddeus Kennedy's an Irish name.

Pause.

Tad It's not the one I started out with.

Pause.

Michael Armstrong. That's my, you know . . .

Bea You're really called Michael Armstrong?

Tad   Yeah.

Bea   Jesus Christ . . . I've been . . . Who the fuck have I been sleeping with for the last six months?

Tad   Me.

Bea   But you're not who I thought you were.

Tad   I am. Essentially I am. It's just the details that are a bit different.

Bea   Details? Is that what you call them?

Tad   Well, you pretend to be middle class and you're not, you pretend your hair's naturally that colour, you talk in an accent that's completely made up –

Bea   That's not the same thing at all –

Tad   Why isn't it?

Bea   You lied to me, that's the difference –

Tad   I omitted a few facts, I never lied about anything –

Bea   But everything about you's a lie –

Tad   Couldn't you look at it like this, I mean, I feel comfortable being Tad, it feels right, it doesn't feel like a lie. Maybe I'm the cultural equivalent of a transsexual. An Irishman trapped in an Englishman's body.

Bea   Oh, don't be so fucking ridiculous.

Tad   Micheál MacLiammóir was a great Irishman and he came from Kensal Rise. He never set foot in Ireland till he was twenty-three.

Bea   I don't understand . . . I mean . . . why?

Tad   I told you, it felt right. And as soon as I started writing in my Irish voice, it felt true, it felt like mine. When I was writing about England, it didn't seem authentic, it's like my identity was liquid, it just ran through my fingers. I couldn't seem to define myself. Plus I couldn't get a fucking thing published. And I was just the same writer. Except I'm better now. I've got a voice now.

Bea You're mad.

Tad I'm not. I'm not mad at all. But I had to tell you, d'you know?

Bea *stares at him.*

Bea If you're from Hull, talk to me in your real voice.

Tad This is my real voice.

Bea You know what I bloody mean.

Tad (*Hull accent*) The rain in Spain falls mainly on the plain. (*Irish accent.*) Now you do your real accent. Go on, give us a blast of the old Geordie.

Bea Losing an accent's nothing like what you've done. You can't equate social mobility with out-and-out deception –

Tad Social mobility my arse –

Bea But what about your parents, your family?

Tad My mother's dead. My dad . . . we never got on . . . he was a complete bastard . . . knocked my mother and me about, you know . . .

Bea So where is he?

Tad In Hull . . . I see him maybe once a year. He's eighty-five, for fuck's sake.

Bea And he's in on this, is he?

Tad   No. He doesn't watch the sort of programmes you get me on. He doesn't read broadsheets. He doesn't have a clue. He thinks writers are a bunch of jessies. But now . . .

Bea   What?

A beat.

Tad   It doesn't matter. I just know I should have told you, that's all.

Bea   Everything I thought about you, everything that makes you what you are has just disintegrated –

Tad   I'm still everything I was before except I'm not Irish, not in the strictest sense of the word –

Bea   But that was what I loved about you –

Tad   Thanks a fucking bunch –

Bea   I mean I loved all the stuff that comes with that – I mean, you're not real –

Tad   I thought I could get away with it, being a writer and all that. You know, I thought, it's a quiet, invisible sort of profession, it's not like being a film star. And that's what it was for years. A few short stories. Novels that never made much of a splash. Eking out a living, with a bit of this and a bit of that. But suddenly I'm all over the papers. The more visible you want me to be the more scary it gets. I kept thinking I'll stop, I'll tell her, I'll get out of this. But it's like a drug, you know? Cars picking you up, make-up people taking all that trouble over you, cameras, applause, it's like slipping into a big warm bath of affirmation and aren't you fucking marvellous. But all the time I'm thinking any minute now the whole lot's going to come down. I'm being launched into the stratosphere and someone is going to fucking recognise me, Bea. And I just want to get on with my work in peace.

Bea *has poured herself a large whisky. She knocks it back.*

I mean, it doesn't change the way I feel about you –

Bea   But those feelings are suspect, for Christ's sake! They come from some fabricated person, I've been in love with a glove puppet –

Tad   It's me. I'm still me.

He goes towards her. She holds out her hand to ward him off.

Bea   No, don't try and be smoochy with me –

Tad   Bea –

Bea   No . . . fuck off . . . d'you know I was going to bake soda farls tomorrow, especially for you, but fuck them, fuck you and your champ and potato cakes, and your Irish stew –

Tad   Bea –

Bea   – and your fucking peat briquettes, fuck you –

Tad   Bea, peat briquettes are a type of fuel –

Bea   – and your pints of plain and bowls of malt, fuck you and your crubeens, whatever they are, your bacon and cabbage, your Celtic twilight bollocks and your poetic soul that's forty shades of green, you treacherous fucking *Yorkshireman –*

She bursts into tears.

And now look, now look what you've done, look at me, I don't do crying, I haven't cried since 1982, you impostor, you shit –

She sobs. **Tad** *watches awkwardly.*

Tad   Bea. My dad's ill. They've given him two months.

Pause. **Bea** *is still crying.*

Bea   What?

Tad   My dad's dying.

Bea (*sobbing*)   Which one? The one in Hull or some surrogate leprechaun?

Tad   My real one. The only one I've got.

Bea   So . . . ? And . . . ?

Tad   I don't like him. I used to hate him. I used to want to kill him. But he's part of me, you know? . . .

Pause.

Bea, I don't know what the fuck to do.

Blackout.

Scene Two

Lights up, later. Two a.m. Spotlight on **Joni** *posing by the chair in her nightdress. Wild applause, wolf-whistles, camera bulbs flashing. Screen images washing over the set. She strikes a series of provocative poses as the applause dies down.*

Joni   Yeah, I'm really really happy that the truth's out at last. Yeah, he gave me this ring. (*She holds out her hand.*) It belonged to his mother, so you know, it seemed right. Right, it's incredible, I know, my first film and I'm nominated for an Oscar, I can't believe it, it's been an amazing year. Well, I've known Tom since I was tiny, so I've never been in awe of him or anything, and getting the film was nothing to do with our relationship because I'd already got the part before all this happened. Yeah, I met Iona a couple of times, and it was really terrible about the car crash and everything, but I think the relationship was more or less over by then. Decapitated. She never knew what hit her. I think I probably helped him to get over it. Well, it takes a bit of getting used to being over here in Beverly Hills with all the palm trees and everything, it's not much like Hammersmith, I can tell you. And getting mobbed by fans and not being able to leave the house. I've had a couple of stalkers, you know, the usual, God it's so boring. I can't go places like the supermarket any more, but we have staff and everything. Would I take my clothes off on film? I think that's a very difficult question, but yes, if the part demanded it –

Lights change abruptly as **Tom** *comes in, still in his bathrobe, clutching his mobile phone and a glass of whisky. He's sniffing, as if he's taken coke, and is obviously mid-conversation.*

Tom –

Tom Joni, sorry, I didn't realise you were still up – .

Joni I was just going to bed, goodnight –

She dashes out, mortified.

Tom Hey, you don't have to go because of me –

He goes back to his conversation.

Sorry, Charlie

He picks up a book, and throws himself down on the cushions. During the conversation, he's trying to snort coke from a line he manages to lay out on the book.

Yeah, he's thrilled. Thinks I'd make a great Padraig. All we need now is a screenplay. But Charlie, listen, I'm calling you because I can't sleep. Have you ever heard of a fetch? (*He looks at his watch.*) It's three a.m. What d'you mean you're going out? You're my agent, you're supposed to make soothing noises when I make irrational calls in the middle of the night. Hold on –

He moves away from the phone, and snorts the line of coke.

No, truly, I'm serious, I'm having a crisis here, I'm in the middle of fucking nowhere, it's colder than North Dakota, and we've had a power failure. I come all this way, to some county I've never heard of, full of people who sound like

Vikings, I've no idea where I am, left of Norway or somewhere, and there's a fetch outside. A fetch . . . It's a spook. It's a doppelgänger and it's in the garden.

Iona appears in her dressing gown with the camera to her eye.

Iona   Tom –

Tom   I am not fucking drunk! Listen to me. Can you imagine anything more horrible than to see someone coming towards you and it's you? . . . No, not you, me . . . No, *I* meet me. *I* run into myself . . . no, you don't come into it at all . . . you're not in this scene OK . . . I'm talking about the fetch . . . I just told you for fuck's sake . . . I'm not in bed, I'm in the living room . . . because it's three a.m. and I don't want to wake Iona . . .

Iona   So stop shouting then –

Tom   You see, you woke her up –

She takes the phone from him. Continuing to film.

Iona   Hi, Charlie, it's me . . . no, he's OK, he's jet-lagged and tired, that's all . . . yes he's warm enough . . . The house has heating, Charlie, we don't have to sleep in our clothes . . . I'm sorry? . . . really . . . ? That sounds pretty unusual . . . yeah, why don't you go on out to dinner . . . boy, you don't know how good that sounds, the sun dipping down over the Pacific, I'm so jealous . . .

Tom   Tell him to call me tomorrow –

Iona   He says to call him tomorrow – OK, goodnight, Charlie . . .

She turns off the phone.

Tom   What did he say? Did he say I was drunk?

Iona   No.

Tom   Did he say I sounded emotional?

Iona   No. He said did you bring cashmere socks because a friend of his went to Scotland and got frostbite and had to have his toe amputated. And cashmere socks would have saved that toe.

She goes.

Tom   Iona?

She doesn't respond. He yells at the top of his voice.

Iona!

Iona *comes back.*

Iona   What?

Tom   D'you think that thing, the fetch? D'you think it ever gets inside the house?

Joni *appears in the doorway wearing her dressing gown and with a joint in her hand.*

Joni   Tom. Can I speak to you a minute?

Iona   It's three a.m., Joni, you should be asleep.

She looks at **Joni**.

Are you smoking dope?

Joni   I'm allowed.

Iona   Are you sure?

Joni *looks at* **Iona**'s *camera and puts the joint behind her back.*

Joni   Don't film me though.

She hovers awkwardly.

I can't get to sleep.

Tom   Me neither.

Joni   Why?

Tom   Just a little jittery, that's all.

She offers him the joint.

Joni, I don't think you should smoke that, you're way too young –

Joni   When you get cross you look exactly like I do when I get cross.

Tom   I do?

Joni   Can I put some music on?

Tom   Sure, but don't you think you should be asleep? –

She goes to the CD and puts on some hip-hop music.

Iona   Joni, I think you should go back to bed, come on, I'm going up –

*She takes **Joni**'s arm but **Joni** shrugs her off.*

Joni   I want to talk to Tom about something.

Iona   OK, I give up on both of you. I'm exhausted.

*She goes out. **Joni** begins to sway to the music.*

Joni   D'you think my skin really is luminous?

Tom   Sure.

Joni   Is it true, all that stuff about reflecting light?

Tom   Probably.

Joni   I really love dancing, don't you?

Tom   Yeah.

Joni   But I'm also quite a spiritual person.

Tom   Right.

Pause. She stops dancing.

Joni   Tom. I know.

Tom   Excuse me?

Joni   I know.

Tom   What?

Joni   It's all right. Mum didn't tell me, I just worked it out.

Tom   Worked what out?

She comes over and tentatively sits at his feet.

Joni   I know you're my dad.

Tom *is taken aback. He sits up.*

Tom   What?

Joni   I know you're my –

Tom   Joni, no, hey, hold on –

Joni   But I know –

Tom   Joni, Philip is your dad –

Joni   It's OK, I know he's not. I don't look like him, I look like you –

Tom   I don't think you do, honey, I think you're just – listen, I'm not your dad, I swear to God I'm not –

Joni   Why are you denying it?

Tom   Because it's not true. I am not your father.

Joni *is confused and embarrassed.*

Joni   But I worked it out! You were in London when I was conceived and I know you were staying with Mum because I found photographs of you with the date on and you have your arms round her, and you look, you look –

Tom   Joni. Listen to me. I am not your father.

Kitty *and* **Bea** *come in.*

Bea   Joni, what are you doing? And what's this bloody awful music that's waking everyone up?

She turns off the music. **Joni** *and* **Tom** *both get up, covered in embarrassment, as if they've been caught out.*

Joni *(tearfully)*   You'll never speak to me again now, will you –

Tom   I will. I promise. It was a mistake, that's all, honey. Now get some sleep.

Bea   What's going on?

Joni *looks at her.*

Joni   Nothing. It's private, OK? It's just a thing between me and Tom, all right?

She goes out.

Kitty   What's she talking about?

Tom   Nothing. Forget it.

Kitty   Were you chatting her up?

Tom   Oh, for Christ's sake, of course I wasn't –

Bea   Of course he wasn't –

Kitty   D'you know somehow that's less convincing coming from a man with an underage sex charge round his neck –

Tom   I was not trying to seduce Joni, or any other young woman –

Kitty   So how come you've got one suing you, and another one practically sitting on your face?

Tom   She was not sitting on my face –

Kitty Only because we walked in before you off –

Tom She thinks I'm her dad, for Christ's sake

Bea What?

Kitty Where did she get that idea from?

Tom Search me.

They both look at **Bea**.

Bea It's nothing to do with me.

Kitty You're not, are you?

Bea Of course he's not.

Tom Of course I'm not.

Kitty Jesus, so you're trying to seduce her and she's thinking she's your daughter. No wonder she's upset –

Bea Kitty –

Tom I wasn't trying to seduce her, how many times d'you want me to say it. Jesus wept, underage girls are not my problem –

Kitty Hah!

Bea Oh, for Christ's sake, Kitty, he wasn't trying to seduce Joni, now will you just forget the whole thing –

Kitty Why are you on his side? Why aren't you defending your daughter's honour?

Bea Because, oh, for God's sake –

Kitty What?

Tom Listen, I don't have any kind of problem with young girls. That is not my problem, OK?

Kitty   So why are they suing you?

Bea *and* **Tom** *look at each other. A considered pause.*

Bea   Men . . . are his problem.

Kitty   What d'you mean, men?

Tom   I fuck them.

Pause.

Kitty (*uncertainly*)   Yeah. And my mother's the Empress of Russia.

Tom   I'm serious.

She looks at **Bea**.

Kitty   Is he serious?

Bea   Yes.

Pause.

Kitty   And you knew this?

Bea   He wouldn't let me tell you, he wouldn't let me tell anyone –

Kitty   So he sleeps with men. Since when?

Tom   Since for ever.

Pause.

Kitty   But you've slept with me.

Bea   He's slept with *you*?

Tom   And I also sleep with men –

Bea   *When* did he sleep with you?

Tom   – which is not an admissible orientation for someone in my position –

Bea   Obviously, he's not, in the past, been the most committed homosexual seeing as he's also slept with me.

Kitty   Jesus Christ, Tom, is there anybody you haven't slept with? Are our pets safe? *When* did he sleep with you?

Bea   Years ago. When we were at college –

Tom   Listen, can we forget about the when and the where –

Kitty   Because that would be so much more convenient for you, wouldn't it. Bea, I can't believe you never told me this –

Tom   Christ, this is a big deal, d'you understand? I come out to my oldest friend and what does she do? She argues about who fucked who when –

Kitty   And what about all this underage girl stuff?

Tom   It's a scam. Iona and Bea cooked it up with my agent.

Kitty   So it's not true? It's just horseshit?

Bea   Well, no, there is a woman –

Tom   I mean, she's real –

Bea   It's just –

Tom   She's an old friend, my yoga teacher. She said she would spin this story about how I broke her heart, it was a fun thing, we laughed about it, she was my beard. And then fuck, what happened, she got carried away, suddenly she's claiming she was sixteen years old, she's making up all sorts of things –

Bea   I think she liked the attention.

Tom   Invented a whole load of shit, a whole scenario that never happened, things we did in bed, hotels we went to, how I picked her up from high school, I mean, you know, she's a fucking yoga teacher, she told me she was on the path to enlightenment–

Bea   When actually she's mad as a bag of snakes, Jesus, I wish you'd let me meet her before you got into this, Tom, I'm a professional, I know a fantasist whan I see one –

Tom   Anyway, it's over, we paid her off. She wanted a nose job, and to go to some ashram in the Hindu Kush because she mistakenly thinks Mel Gibson once hung out there. Let's hope she fucking stays.

Kitty   And what does Iona get out of this set-up?

Tom   Iona doesn't really go for men –

Kitty   Of course not. How stupid of me to think she did.

Tom   She gets to make a movie –

Kitty   Which will be bullshit from start to finish –

Tom   I play straight leading men, Kitty.

Bea   He can't afford to come out.

Kitty   Let's just get this right. You're bisexual. You've always been bisexual?

Tom   Yeah. Except I'm increasingly inclined towards, you know . . .

Kitty   Gaydom.

Tom   Yeah.

Kitty   But you're going to suppress this, for the sake of your career?

Tom   That's what I've always done.

Kitty   For Christ's sake, Tom –

Tom   We're talking about Hollywood here. We have gay rights, we have gay pride, we have gay marriages, but we don't have gay movie stars.

Kitty   James Dean.

Tom   You're allowed to come out if you're dead. Or British.

Kitty   Tom, this is a hall of mirrors –

Tom   Listen, I like women, you know that. I don't even mind having sex with them. It's just I also like having sex with men, and stories get around. Hence the young girl.

Kitty   I can't believe you went along with this, Bea. And you never told me –

Bea   He wouldn't let me, it's not my fault –

Kitty   Why didn't you trust me?

Tom   It's a fire that needs to be contained. There was no need for you to know –

Kitty   Excuse me –

Bea   D'you know something? I need to lie down. Believe me, this is the least of my worries right now. Christmas isn't really panning out that well for me at the moment. I'll be in the spare room at the back if there's anything else you need to get off your chest.

Kitty   Why aren't you sleeping with Tad?

Bea   Because we're not actually on speaking terms.

She goes out.

Kitty   Can I just sort something out here? Sorry to bother you with the vulgarity of the when and where, but when you slept with me –

Tom   Listen, things got pretty wild afterwards, you know
. . . I mean, I was kind of out of control and making a
picture and I guess . . . I'm sorry, OK. I should have called
you.

Kitty   I'm surprised you even remember it.

Tom   Oh, come on. It was a whole week.

Kitty   Ten days.

Tom   Yeah, well, you didn't call me either.

Kitty   You didn't give me your number.

Tom   You're kidding me? Why didn't you get it from Bea
or someone?

Kitty *looks at him.*

Kitty   Hi, I bumped into Tom in New York, we got
ripped and spent a week in bed together. Now I need his
phone number to find out why he never calls me.

Tom   Were you really waiting for me to call?

Kitty   Well, it would have been polite, you know? And
because even if I did have your number, I couldn't have
called you anyway.

Tom   Why not?

Kitty   Because you're Tom Cavallero.

Tom   We've known each other for twenty years, for
Christ's sake. Twenty-three, to be accurate.

Kitty   And in all that time you never told me you were
gay –

Tom   Half gay –

Kitty   What I'm saying is you're a movie star. I don't
know how to be with you. I don't know how I'm supposed

to behave. I do angry, because it's better than doing embarrassment.

Tom   You should have called me.

Kitty   I should have called you?

Tom   Kitty, this is getting circular –

Kitty   Fifteen years ago I tried calling you in LA. I got your secretary who said, 'How did you get this number?' When I said I was your friend she said, 'I'm sorry but you don't appear on Tom's list of bona fide people, I'm afraid I can't pass on your message.' Are you surprised I didn't try and track you down this time?

Tom   Was her name Maribel, this secretary?

Kitty   I've no idea.

Tom   Maribel I had to fire. She refused to put my mother through. Plus she had this weird personal hygiene thing, she was always cleaning her hands on these anti-bacterial wipes, and disinfecting the telephone. Also she stole my clothing, like socks and stuff. After I fired her I ran into her in a bookstore and she was wearing my jacket. Can you believe that?

Kitty   Your nose is bleeding.

Tom   Shit.

He wipes it.

Has it gone?

Kitty   Yeah.

Tom   Listen, I just want to say –

Kitty   Forget it, OK, it was three years ago, it's stupid.

Pause.

It's just . . . the reason I'm here is I've had a fight with
Duncan.

Tom *looks at her.*

Tom   Who's Duncan?

Kitty   He's my fucking husband, how many times do I
have to tell you this?

Tom   OK, OK, I'm sorry –

Kitty   We went out to a party one night and got, you
know, that sort of drunk when you can sort out the Balkans
and dance like Ginger Rogers. I thought, hey, I'm invincible
and in love, this man understands me like no one on earth,
let's have no secrets. So in a moment of champagne-fuelled
love and honesty, I told him I'd had this thing with you. I
thought I could tell him anything and he'd understand. I
thought he loved me enough. And instead he just went very
quiet, like I'd thrown a bucket of water over him. He
worked out that it happened just after I'd met him. And
instead of us spending a quiet Christmas together in
London, he's gone off to some bloody civil war to punish
me. He hasn't even phoned.

Tom *gropes around for his phone.*

Tom   You want me to call him? What's his number? I'll
call him and tell him it's OK, I'm a faggot, how would that
be?

Kitty   I don't know why I told him. I didn't think he went
in for jealousy. Jesus. I spend one week with you three years
ago and my whole life goes down the toilet –

Tom   Kitty, I'm not taking the rap for this. You told your
husband you slept with a movie star –

Kitty   I did nothing of the sort –

Tom He'll get over it. He'll come back. If he doesn't he's an asshole. Fuck him.

Kitty You probably would actually. He's quite handsome.

Tom Listen, I'm sorry I didn't get in touch. I've been, you know, under a lot of pressure lately. I've been worried about a lot of things, my career for one . . . you know, there's all these young guys coming through, all these focused Scientology types, I mean, I don't know where to . . . I don't know how to . . .

Kitty What?

Tom I don't know.

Pause.

I don't know how to live. That's it. I don't know how to live. D'you think I'm insane?

Kitty You're a homosexual pretending to be straight. To me, that's insane. No wonder you're miserable. I mean, look at the state of you –

Tom Kitty, are you happy?

Kitty Of course I'm not.

Tom Why?

Kitty I just told you why. Duncan's sulking in the middle of a civil war. If he gets killed it'll be my fault, for sleeping with you and telling him about it. Also my job's so stupid I could die.

Tom Have you seen my last movie? Stupid is flattering.

Kitty I'm ashamed. I'm embarrassed. I host a programme that does dramatic reconstructions of terrible accidents, and how people escaped by the skin of their teeth. It is entirely without merit.

Tom   Right. It's not good then?

Kitty   It's banal, anecdotal and mindless. At best it panders to curiosity, and at worst voyeurism. Its original title was 'Close Shaves'. Then they discovered a porn mag with the same name. I'm earning a fortune.

Tom   So, that's why you're doing it.

Kitty   No. I lost my nerve for the other stuff. I was doing a report from one of the new republics from the ex-Soviet Union. Civil disturbances, looting, snipers, mortars, reports of torture. All par for the course. Then this day I was filming with a camera crew and I realised the soldiers behind us were beating up a bunch of young boys for us. Because we had a camera. Not just a punch and a slap. They were beating them unconscious with rifle butts, with their boots. Blood was spurting from noses, teeth flying. And the soldiers were shouting: 'Look, this is what we do to looters, this is how we treat them, put this in your report.' And the guys just kept on filming. I said, no, stop, stop filming, they're going to kill them. But they didn't stop. They said it was reporting but it wasn't, it was something else. It went out on televisions all over the world as actuality, and what it was, was a performance. Afterwards they told me I'd copped out, that I'd lost my nerve. I don't know. Maybe I have. Anyway, they all got awards for that report. And I just felt confused. But if I didn't have the stomach for that stuff, I sure as hell don't have the stomach for what I'm doing at the moment. And I'm supposed to be filming the day after tomorrow.

Tom   D'you know something? You're the realest person I know. Apart from Iona. No. You're even more real than she is.

Kitty   Tom, when was the last time you touched base with 'real'? Iona's a lesbian pretending to be your girlfriend.

Tom Actually I think she's asexual. But one thing, right, about being, you know, in the weird position I'm in, is you get to fuck a lot of people –

Kitty Thank you, that makes me feel very valued –

Tom No, listen to me, you get to fuck, like, anyone.

Kitty And this is supposed to make me feel better, is it?

Tom No, I don't count you in this. What I mean is that I find it depressing. You know most of them will do almost anything, they'd do back flips with an iguana if I asked them, because I'm Tom Cavallero. Whoever the fuck he is.

Kitty Tom, you wanted this more than anything. At college, all you were ever going to be was famous.

Tom I know. I thought the alternative was a kind of living death. To live your whole life and not be known. Like obscurity, what's the point?

Kitty Well, there's no obscurity for you now even if you want it. No matter what you do or where you go, someone, one day, will say, Hey, didn't you used to be Tom Cavallero? And then you'll be a has-been which really is a living death. There's no escape.

Tom This guy I slept with, sorry to get back to this but it bugs me, right, this one guy, he said, 'Your dick's much smaller than I thought it was going to be,' and I said, 'What d'you mean, it's a completely normal size, what's wrong with it?' And he said, 'I know but I'm used to seeing you on screen where your head's like fifteen feet across, so you know . . . '

Kitty Why d'you sleep with these people?

Tom Because I can.

Pause.

Because I'm bored. I don't know.

Pause.

You get jaded, you know? You get bored with people who'll just do anything for you. You want a challenge or something. I went out with this woman once who wanted me to do really bizarre things with an electric toothbrush, right –

Kitty   Like what?

Tom   The batteries were flat, so we never did it. But she bossed me around, you know? She ordered me, do this, do that, and I kind of liked it, it was different. But outside of that she wasn't very interesting, plus she was a really bad actress, which kind of turned me off. We split and she sold the story to the *National Enquirer*, which made it sound like it was me who had the thing about domestic appliances. She got killed skateboarding down a freeway with half a ton of prescription drugs inside her, so I guess there's some justice.

Kitty   The thing is, Tom, you have everything you ever wanted.

Tom   There's this guy ghost-writing my autobiography, right –

Kitty   What?

Tom   Yeah, I know, listen, it's just one of those things, and I didn't have time to do it myself –

Kitty   Is he going to mention the men at all, or is he just writing a complete fiction?

Tom   What do you think? So anyway, he gets to the final chapter, right, and I've read the other ones by this time, and I think, hey, I think I could get the hang of this guy's style, so I write the final chapter myself.

Kitty So?

Tom So I've mastered the style of a ghost-writer, who's pretending to be me. Basically, I'm a man pretending to be a man who's pretending to be me. It completely scrambled my brain.

Kitty So you thought you'd better take half a ton of cocaine to unscramble it –

Tom Could you be sympathetic for like a nanosecond?

Kitty I'm sorry for you. Your life is unbearable, it's hell. How you struggle through I don't know, maybe you'd like an honorary knighthood for your services to recreational drug use –

Tom Listen, I came here for some . . . I don't know . . . some . . .

Kitty What?

Tom Have you ever seen a sign on an old building that says 'Ancient Lights'?

Kitty Yes.

Tom I saw it twenty years ago on a house on the banks of the Thames. It's kind of haunted me. It's so poetic. It's so mythic.

Kitty It just means you can't build another house within fifty yards because you'll block the light to the windows. It's a form of building regulation.

Silence.

Tom You're kidding me?

Kitty No.

Tom Oh my God. That is just so . . . Jesus . . . you're telling me that for twenty years I've been haunted by a building regulation?

Kitty What did you think it meant?

Tom I don't know. I just thought it was so . . . English and historical and mysterious. Those words have such resonance. Ancient Lights. I though they were about place, and rootedness, and belonging. Like the way Tad carries his Irishness so lightly because it's who he is, it's his history. I thought those words had some atavistic meaning that only the English could truly understand. They're part of what brings me back here.

Pause.

This is terrible.

Kitty Sorry.

Tom That's OK.

He starts to cry. **Kitty** *is appalled.*

Kitty Tom, look, I'm sorry. I mean, I could be wrong. In fact I am, I'm wrong, I'm completely wrong about this.

Tom You're not. I know you're not.

Kitty I didn't realise it would be so upsetting.

Tom Forget it. It doesn't matter . . .

He wipes his eyes. Silence.

You're a Catholic, right?

Kitty Lapsed.

Tom Same here. When you were a kid, did they ever tell you what heaven was going to be like?

Kitty   We'd sit at God's right hand for ever and ever, and there'd be no more tears and no more want, and everyone would be happy more or less permanently. And bliss. We'd all be lolling around in great vats of it, ad infinitum.

Tom   No more want. Everything you ever desired or dreamed of. Permanent fucking bliss. Just one thing wrong here.

Kitty   Several actually.

Tom   I mean, the nature of bliss is that it's, you know, fleeting. Otherwise it's just . . .

Kitty   What?

Tom   Completely and utterly intolerable . . . D'you know what I mean?

Blackout.

Scene Three

Seven a.m. Christmas morning. Same room. **Bea** *is straightening up the room in her dressing gown, beating something in a bowl. Christmas-morning carols are playing on the radio.* **Tad** *comes in.*

Tad   Happy Christmas.

Bea   Morning.

Tad   You're speaking to me then?

Silence.

Can I do anything?

Bea   You could spontaneously combust. That would solve all my problems at one fell swoop.

Tad   Right.

She beats whatever's in the bowl furiously. Silence. **Tad** *is stranded, awkward.*

Bea   So. You asked me what you should do.

Tad   I did, yeah.

Bea   Go to Hull. Spend Christmas with your dad.

Pause.

Tad   What?

Bea   Have lunch and go.

Tad   But –

Bea   There won't be another Christmas. You won't have another chance.

Tad   I don't want to make my peace with him, if that's what you mean. That's just bollocky sentimental crap.

Bea   He's dying. Swallow your pride.

Tad   I can't.

Bea   You can.

Tad   I don't want to.

Bea   Take the leap. Think of it as making peace with yourself.

Tad   Say goodbye to him, and say goodbye to Michael Armstrong you mean?

Bea   I didn't say that. You did.

Pause.

Also, Tad, I'd quite like you out of my hair for a while.

Tad   Ah. Right.

Bea   I need a bit of time to get used to this . . . new development, you know?

Tad   I can't really blame you, I suppose.

Pause.

Bea   What was he like, this Michael Armstrong?

Tad   Jesus, we were two peas in a pod. Anyone would have taken us for brothers. Same sense of humour. Same mole, here. Same knocked-about mother who wanted the best for us.

Bea   So what's the difference between you and him?

Tad   I'm the successful one.

Pause.

Bea   When you see your dad, who are you going to be?

Tad   What? Who am I going to be? . . . Me . . . I'm going to be me.

Bea   And who the fuck is that?

Tad   I usually kind of morph into Michael by degrees, you know what I mean? I can manage such a smooth transition now, I can hardly see the join myself.

Pause.

If I go, will you still want me when I get back?

Pause.

Bea   I might.

Tad   You'll be living with a liar and a conman.

Silence.

On the other hand, no one else needs to know that.

Bea   And what the world doesn't know doesn't count?

Tad   Something like that. The work's what counts.

Bea   What gets me, is that you're a brilliant writer and it's based on what? Thin air.

Tad   All writing's based on thin air.

Bea   There's no need to take it to extremes.

Tad   D'you think you could live with the fact that I've invented myself?

Bea   Fuck, I don't know. On the other hand, why not? I'd be out of a job if people didn't reinvent themselves.

Pause.

But I also don't want to lose you. I know that's pathetic, I know it is, but I don't. There, I've admitted it. If I was the person people think I am, I'd throw you out on the street. But I can't imagine my life without you, it's too bleak to contemplate. My heart drops like a stone when I think about it. I've done years of being alone. All those empty Sundays that last three weeks. I'm in too deep now.

Tad   Maybe in the night, you know, with your legs wrapped around me in the dark . . . only you and I will know what we know . . .

Bea   You're never going to tell anyone else . . . are you?

Tad   No . . . it's our secret . . .

Bea   But when we make love, I'm going to call you Michael . . .

Tad   Wouldn't that be very confusing?

Bea   Just for those moments I want to be sure of who you are. And for you to be sure too. When I call you Michael, and you respond, I'll know you're mine.

She kisses him, long and deep.

Michael . . .

Tad   I think I'd prefer Mike.

Bea   And I want you to take me seriously.

Tad   OK. Sorry. Michael. OK. You can call me that under the duvet.

Bea   It's our secret.

Tad   Of course if I ever, you know . . . let you down in any way, you could . . .

Bea *looks him in the eye.*

Bea   Yes. I could.

Tad   Not that you're blackmailing me or anything.

Bea   As if.

A beat.

Tad   So. I'm going to Hull then?

Bea   How will you feel about him dying?

Tad   I've been thinking a lot about that.

Bea   Yes, I know.

Tad   I think what I think is this: that death's not just something that happens at the end of your life, it's something that happens from moment to moment. Every moment's a birth and a death. I'm not the man I was twenty years ago. My dad's not the man he was. From moment to moment, we start again. Maybe if I bear that in mind, I'll resist the temptation to punch him.

Blackout.

Scene Four

Christmas Day. Four p.m. A post-prandial tableau: **Tom** *and*
Kitty *have crashed out on the cushions. Everyone is wearing paper
hats out of crackers.* **Bea** *is clearing away wrapping paper, glasses
and general detritus.* **Joni** *is sitting in the kitchen chair wearing a new
leather coat and looking at herself critically in a hand mirror.* **Iona**'s
camera is on the floor with a pile of videotapes.

Joni   I've decided what I want to do when I leave school,
Mum. If the band doesn't work out, I mean, it probably
won't, but anyway, I'd rather be an actress, or if not an
actress, I'll do the breakfast programme on the television or
something like that, you know, be a personality, but I just
know in my heart, Mum, that what I want more than
anything else, right, is to be so famous I can't leave the
house.

Bea   Could you pass me those glasses please?

Joni   More famous than Tom. Much more. Tom is going
to be asking me for my autograph. I might give him a wave
from my stretch limo as I glide past. Just think. You'll be the
mother of a famous child, won't it be great? You might even
get quite famous yourself because of me, and people will
want to see the bedroom I slept in and things like that; I
might even let you be my manager, except I'll probably
have to live in America, God, I can't wait –

She smiles at herself in the mirror.

D'you think Dad would give me the money to have my
teeth straightened?

Bea   No.

Joni *gets up sulkily and begins to sort through the videos on the
floor.*

Bea   Kitty . . .

Kitty *shifts slightly.*

Kitty   What . . . ?

Bea   You won't sleep tonight if you don't wake up now. And you've got a car coming for you in the morning.

Kitty   I'm not going.

She turns over.

Bea   Not going where?

Kitty   Filming. I'm not going.

Bea   What d'you mean? Have they cancelled or something?

Kitty   No. I have.

Bea   What are you talking about?

Kitty   I'm breaking my contract. They'll have to sue me. Fuck them.

Bea   Are you out of your mind?

Kitty *sits up blearily.*

Kitty   Actually I might have to say that. I might have to claim insanity. D'you know any good doctors who might vouch for the parlous state of my mental health?

Bea   Kitty, you can't break your contract. It's completely unprofessional.

Kitty   Watch me.

She picks up a bottle of water and takes a long swig.

One more series of whoops I nearly got killed, and d'you know what I'll be doing next? Pet programmes. Cute pets get cured of impetigo. No thanks. I'm too old.

Tad *comes in with a suitcase.*

Tad   I suppose I'd better get going then.

Joni (*still sorting through the videos*)   Bye. I hope your dad gets better.

Kitty   Are you sure you can get a flight on Christmas Day?

Tad   I'm driving –

Bea   There's a ferry first thing –

Tad   Six o'clock.

Kitty   So where will you stay tonight?

Bea   His brother.

Tad   Yeah, my brother.

Tom *stirs. He's still wearing his paper hat.*

Tom   My neck . . . what time is it?

Bea   It's still Christmas Day. Tad's going to see his father.

Tom   Oh. Right. Right.

He gets up unsteadily and picks up a bottle of whisky. Pours himself a large one.

Good to meet you, Tad. Give my love to the old country, will you.

Tad   Right. I will.

Tom   I can't wait to make this movie.

Joni *has slipped a cassette into the video recorder.*

Tad   Sure it'll be great. We'll have great craic.

Tom   Excuse me?

Tad   Craic. You know. Craic.

Tom   Yeah, right. Great. I –

He breaks off as the video suddenly whirrs into action, the sound up way too high.

Bea   Joni, what are you doing –

Joni   It's just one of Iona's tapes –

Tom   Where the fuck did you get that from?

Joni   It was lying on the floor.

They all stare in horror at the screen: **Tom** *slumped in the living room, coked out of his head, talking to his agent on the phone the night before. He looks appalling.*

Tom (*on tape*)   . . . I am not fucking drunk! Listen to me. Can you imagine anything more horrible than to see someone coming towards you and it's you? . . . No, not you, me . . . (*etc.*)

Kitty   Oh dear, I hope she's going to edit that out.

Bea   Joni, that's enough, turn it off please –

Joni   Ah, Mum –

Tom *is transfixed.*

Tom   Jesus Christ. Is that what I look like?

Tad   Listen, I think I'd better get going –

Kitty   It was the middle of the night, Tom, no one looks good at three in the morning.

Tom   I don't think I need this . . .

Bea   Joni, turn it off, for Christ's sake –

Tom   No, no, no, no –

He goes to the video and wrenches it out. He kneels on the floor and tears the tape from the casing in shining black coils.

Bea   Tom –

Bea *and* **Kitty** *try to gather up the tape as* **Iona** *comes in. She looks at* **Tom** *in horror.*

Iona   What are you doing?

Bea   I don't think he liked that particular bit of film.

Tom   I'm sorry, Iona, I don't think this movie's such a good idea any more –

Tom *has now started on the other tapes. There are coils of black tape everywhere.* **Iona** *tries to wrench them from him.*

Iona   Tom, stop it, please, don't fucking do this –

Bea   Joni, go upstairs to your room –

Joni   Ah, Mum –

Bea   Now!

She goes.

Tom   It was a stupid idea, Iona, I look a complete asshole –

Iona   I was going to edit that stuff out. We had a deal, you promised –

Iona *tries to wrest the tapes from him. He pushes her over.*

Bea   Tom, you made your point, stop it –

Iona   This is three months' work, Tom –

Tom (*still shredding and tearing*)   Let's just forget the whole thing. Make another film, make ten other films, but leave me out. I want this stuff burned, I want it obliterated –

Kitty   Tom –

Iona   They don't want some other film, they want this one, they want a film about you, you asshole, Jesus, Tom, the whole point of everything is that the film's about you. It was your idea, for Christ's sake –

Tom   And it's my idea to stop right now. OK? It's over. The project is abandoned.

Iona   Tom –

Tom   I said it's over!

Iona *begins to cry. She picks up an armful of tape.*

Iona   I can't believe you've done this . . . all my work, wasted –

Tad   Look, I'm really sorry to butt in like this but I have to go –

Iona *gets up, weeping.*

Iona   Tom, you're an asshole.

She goes out. Silence.

Tom   I guess she's a little put out.

Bea   Will she be OK?

He sits down on the cushions.

Tom   Fuck knows. She'll probably write a story for the *National Enquirer* about how I ruined her career.

He picks up a handful of tape and tries to shred it.

So, here I am. This is me. *Cinéma-vérité.*

Bea   Tom –

Tom   D'you ever look in the mirror and you don't recognise the person looking back at you?

Tad   Look, I'm off, right? I really am this time. Great to meet you all, but, you know, my dad and everything –

Kitty   Sorry, Tad. I'm sorry about your dad. Give my love
to Dublin.

Tad   Sure.

She kisses him. He shakes **Tom***'s hand.*

Bye, Tom. Sorry about the er . . .

He looks at the mess.

Anyway. Bye. See you.

Tom   See you in the Emerald Isle.

Tad   Great.

Bea   I'll see you out.

She goes out. **Tom** *starts to roll a joint. The telephone rings.* **Tom**
looks round to see where the noise is coming from.

Kitty   It's OK, it's mine.

It continues to ring.

Tom   Aren't you going to answer it?

Kitty   No. You are.

It continues to ring. She finds it and hands it to **Tom**.

Tell them I've left for London, and I didn't seem too
well –

She picks up the phone and thrusts it at **Tom**.

Tom   Hi? . . . No . . . this is a friend of hers . . . she must
have left it behind . . . no, she left . . . maybe two, three hours
ago? . . . I think she said London . . . she said she wasn't
feeling too good . . . OK . . . I will . . . OK . . . bye . . .

He turns off the phone.

Kitty   Tom, you saved my life.

Tom   This morning I ruined it. My, how times change.

Bea *comes back, throws herself down on the cushions and the reels of tape.*

Bea   Jesus, what a fucking Christmas, the whole thing's been a bloody disaster –

Tom   Bea, it's been great, what are you talking about. Apart from Tad's old man. And Iona. And the film.

Bea   Why did you do that, Tom? Iona's in bits.

Tom   I didn't like what I saw.

Kitty   You wanted reality and that's what you got.

Tom   Fuck it. Fuck reality. You know what I saw there that I've never seen before?

Kitty   Tom Cavallero on screen without make-up.

Tom   No.

Pause.

I looked camp. I looked fucking camp.

Bea   You don't look camp, Tom –

Tom   Say what you like, I know what I saw.

He lights up the joint and hands it to her. Throughout the following scene the joint is passed round.

And I never want to see it again. But I have this horrible feeling I will. Tell me, do I sound camp to you? Give me the truth. Do I sound like a screamer?

Kitty   No. You do not sound like a screamer.

Tom   I don't know whether I believe you.

Bea   You do not sound camp.

Tom   You don't detect a kind of inflection? A little louche thing? Just a hint of something around the shoulders, that tiny facial quirk which says –

Kitty   No. Have some of this.

She hands him the joint. He takes a drag.

Tom   OK.

Pause.

Even my teeth looked gay –

Bea   Well, you are gay for Christ's sake –

Tom   I looked irrational, raving, drunk. And camp.

Kitty   Can we change the subject?

Tom   OK, hey, what a truly great Christmas –

Bea   Oh, shut up –

Tom   Seriously. Apart from fetches and power failures, and the realisation that I'm turning into Liberace –

Kitty   Stop –

Tom   – it's great being here with the snow and all. Christmas never feels real in LA. It's great being in the place where Christmas actually began.

Kitty   That was Bethlehem.

Tom   Yeah, but if we were in Israel it wouldn't feel right, would it? It'd be pretty much like LA, which like I said just doesn't get when it comes to Christmas. You have to be here with the log fire and the real tree and the thatched cottages with all the snow on them.

Kitty   There aren't any thatched cottages up here.

Tom   I've seen them.

Kitty Where?

Tom Everywhere.

Bea You imagined it. There are no thatched cottages up here, period.

Tom This is England for Christ's sake.

Bea You only get thatch further south, Tom.

Tom Jesus . . . Maybe my therapist is right. He says I create realities.

Bea *hands on the joint.*

Bea Neurolinguistic programming.

Kitty What?

Bea It's a type of therapy.

Kitty Yeah, but what does it do?

Bea No idea.

Tom Freudian. Kleinian. Episcopalian. Tried them all.

Kitty Go back to Catholicism. The priests have the best outfits. Greek Orthodox, even better. Great outfits and great beards.

Tom But how d'you get . . . you know . . . the thing . . . faith . . .

Kitty Actually Bea, you could found your own church. The First Church of Christ the Chef.

Bea I wish I did have a religion.

Kitty A different job would do me.

Bea I'm serious.

Kitty   So am I. Look at what we all do. What is the point of any of it?

Tom   Iridology. Healers. Bio-feedback. I had someone read my feet once. Can you believe that? Read my feet, I want to know the answers to the big questions, go on, read my feet and tell me, I know it's all there somewhere.

Bea   What did they have to say for themselves?

Tom   Oh, you know. You're basically a good person, but sometimes people take advantage of you. Oh and your kidneys are fucked. Thank you that'll be three hundred dollars.

Bea   Channelling. Tibetan chanting. Fire-walking.

Tom   Done them all. Psychosynthesis.

Bea   What's that?

Tom   I can't remember. The therapist was called Skippy.

Kitty   You went to a therapist called Skippy?

Tom   My judgement wasn't good at the time. That's why I was in therapy.

Bea   Was she any use?

Tom   What do you think? I've tried my body's a temple low sodium drug-free spring water organic fruit and jogging routine but it got so I could imagine how clean my intestines were and I was frightened to eat anything in case I messed them up. Plus I even bored myself. I only really start functioning after I'm three beers in.

Bea   So where to now?

Kitty   In the old days, we'd have joined the International Marxists or something.

Bea   Well, you would.

Tom   I don't know. Buddhism. What d'you think?

Kitty   You'd be crap at Buddhism. You have to live in the moment which is not possible if you're turning your whole life into a major motion picture. Plus for you, almost every moment is a lie.

Tom   Get over it, Kitty. I have a friend who says that golf's very Zen if you do it right. What d'you think?

Kitty   Everything's very Zen if you do it right.

Bea *begins to giggle.*

Bea   I set up this interview for you, Tom, and I had to pretend you wouldn't answer any questions about the underage girl thing, and they got so fed up, so when you apparently relent mid-interview, they're going to think it's such a scoop.

Tom   Hey, I have the whole spiel worked out – 'D'you know this woman's been hounding me? She sent me a paperweight with her pubic hair set inside it. She sat in some uncooked dough, baked it and sent me the results: a loaf of bread in the shape of her vagina. And now she's suing me?' Actually, I didn't make that up, someone did that to me once.

Kitty   That is disgusting.

Bea   Are you really breaking your contract, Kitty?

Kitty   Yep. I'm going to sort things out with Duncan. Even if I have to go to Africa to do it. Then, I don't know. Take it from there. Find some work that makes some sense. If you don't have religion, work's all you've got.

Bea   That's depressing.

Kitty   It is if you do what we do.

Bea   Children. Children are what's important. And lovers and friends and families.

Tom   But just sometimes, you want a little bit of transcendence, you know. I thought being a movie star would do it.

Bea   Doesn't it?

Tom   Do I look like I'm transcending anything?

Bea   No. Do I?

Tom   You're a great cook. You're a great organiser.

Bea   That'll look really great on my headstone. What a summing-up: Beatrice Davies, a good organiser. She went to a lot of parties. Fuck.

Kitty   Kitty Percival, she made some terrible television shows.

Tom   Tom Cavallero. Briefly famous.

Kitty   Ah well. Forty-three next birthday. Soon be dead.

Bea   Tad says death's a process, not an event.

Pause.

Tom   Shit. I guess it is.

Kitty*'s phone rings again. They ignore it.*

Tom   Shall I roll another joint?

Bea   Yeah, why not.

He starts to do so. The phone continues to ring.

Tom   It was a dark and windy night. Thomas Earlby was walking his dog across the moors at around five o'clock in the evening, when the dog suddenly stopped, cowering and whimpering and giving little uncertain barks. And Earlby looked up and saw a figure walking towards him with a strange lantern the colour of moonlight.

The phone stops ringing. As **Tom** *talks, a huge image of him (back projection) begins to develop on the walls behind him.*

And the strange thing was that this figure made no sound as it came towards him across the frozen ground. And as it got nearer, Earlby was rooted to the spot, for the man standing before him was his own self, white-faced and gaunt, and beckoning to him, like this . . . Earlby turned on his heels and fled. When he reached home, shocked and shaken, he told his wife and his father what he'd seen out there on the moors, and his father turned white, and got up from the table. He went upstairs without a word. And the next morning, Thomas Earlby was dead . . .

By now the image of **Tom** *fills the back of the stage. Fade down lights, leaving only the image. Bring up John Martyn music. Fade down image.*

Methuen Drama Modern Plays

include work by

Edward Albee
Jean Anouilh
John Arden
Margaretta D'Arcy
Peter Barnes
Sebastian Barry
Brendan Behan
Dermot Bolger
Edward Bond
Bertolt Brecht
Howard Brenton
Anthony Burgess
Simon Burke
Jim Cartwright
Caryl Churchill
Complicite
Noël Coward
Lucinda Coxon
Sarah Daniels
Nick Darke
Nick Dear
Shelagh Delaney
David Edgar
David Eldridge
Dario Fo
Michael Frayn
John Godber
Paul Godfrey
David Greig
John Guare
Peter Handke
David Harrower
Jonathan Harvey
Iain Heggie
Declan Hughes
Terry Johnson
Sarah Kane
Charlotte Keatley
Barrie Keeffe

Howard Korder
Robert Lepage
Doug Lucie
Martin McDonagh
John McGrath
Terrence McNally
David Mamet
Patrick Marber
Arthur Miller
Mtwa, Ngema & Simon
Tom Murphy
Phyllis Nagy
Peter Nichols
Sean O'Brien
Joseph O'Connor
Joe Orton
Louise Page
Joe Penhall
Luigi Pirandello
Stephen Poliakoff
Franca Rame
Mark Ravenhill
Philip Ridley
Reginald Rose
Willy Russell
Jean-Paul Sartre
Sam Shepard
Wole Soyinka
Simon Stephens
Shelagh Stephenson
Peter Straughan
C. P. Taylor
Theatre Workshop
Sue Townsend
Judy Upton
Timberlake Wertenbaker
Roy Williams
Snoo Wilson
Victoria Wood

Lightning Source UK Ltd.
Milton Keynes UK
UKOW030256090212

186956UK00004B/5/P